MW01077807

O.S.A.S

TRUTH OR COUNTERFEIT

Can I commit suicide and go to heaven?

Are my future sins forgiven?

Can salvation be lost?

Jose De La Rosa

Write to:
Jose De La Rosa
1620 Buford Hwy. Suite #113
Buford, GA 30518
or Email to: info@faithpublishers.com

ISBN-10: 1548408107

ISBN-13: 978-1548408107

First Printing—July 2017

Cover designed by Jose De La Rosa

Edited and Proofread by Joseph A. De La Rosa, and Keila M. De La Rosa

Printed in the United States of America

All names, pronouns, and associated names of God the Father, God the Son, and God the Holy Spirit are in capital letters.

The name satan and associated names are not capitalized.

Dedicated to the love of my life, Keila, my friend, a true warrior of faith and companion in ministry, to my children Keise and Joseph, you are a special treasure to me, my inheritance from God; I bless you, love you, and thank God for you.

Acknowledgments

I want to give my sincere gratitude to *Iglesia Mas Que Vencedores,* to Pastor Sarah Gronau de Jiménez (Mamá Sarita), and to Enrique Jiménez, thank you for your inspiration, support and tenderness; may the Lord give you a long life, to Moises Sifren, and Lesley De La Rosa, thank you for your friendship and support, to my wife Keila M. De La Rosa for her cooperation and insights in this book, to my father and mother in Law Damian and Julia Mercedes, thank you for your prayer, to Daniel and Damaris Medina, my nephews Josias and Miqueas thank you for your love and support, to Pedro Williams and wife Raiza Williams thank you for your support, to my spiritual daughter Evangelista (Jackie) Rodriguez for your love and faithfulness, to Richard Horne, Jr. author of *The Making of a Trailblazer*, and his wife Renda Horne author of *Seven Years in Egypt*, and *Happy Is Me!* Thank you for your inspiration, encouragement, and support.

CONTENTS

Preface

Dear friend, first I would like to welcome you to receive new tools to fight the deceitfulness and spiritual decay of these last days. I also want to dedicate this book to those who are confused by the different teachings that pretend to have a new revelation from God that brings an easy gospel. In this book I will be dealing with one of the most popular topics among Christian denominations today: Once Saved Always Saved. This topic has been one of my main projects for the last four years since my wife and I met with a believer who suddenly began to ask questions about salvation. I noticed that she was sincere in her desire to know about this subject; she was really looking for answers. Her church, a mega church in the state of Georgia is teaching (Once Saved Always Saved, and Eternal Assurance, Once Justified Always Justified). Since that time, I have felt compelled to bringing responses not just to this dear sister but to the many believers who are in contact with this teaching. But the Lord put a greater burden on my life when I understood the danger of the real agenda of this false teaching. This teaching is suggesting and even assuring that the believer could commit suicide and still go to heaven. In this book I will present the proofs of how this teaching is false and how suicide was not, and it is not an option for believers. I will also provide the stories of believers in the Bible and how they remained in obedience to God even in the middle of afflictions. Here you will find many answers regarding O.S.A.S. and plenty material that will help you develop your understanding regarding this subject so that you can help others. I encourage you to come with a humble heart to learn through the light of the word of God and to yield to the Holy Spirit. In my personal experience, every time that I found a doctrine that I can't quite understand, I do what the Bereans did to verify the teachings of Apostle Paul. Please open your heart and let the Holy Spirit guide you in this journey of the Spirit to equip you for saving many from eternal damnation. I declare that God is touching your life right now to receive what God has for you in this book.

Let us agree upon five things before we go any further. If we can agree upon these five things, then we can work together to correct anything that is not in line with the word of God.

Do you agree that we love God?

Do you agree that He is our Father?

Do you agree that Jesus is Lord?

Do you agree that the Holy Spirit is God?

Do you accept that the Bible is the inspired, infallible, and eternal word of God?

If we agree in these truths then we can study the word of God together, removing from our lives anything that contradicts the word of God. The word of God is perfect; we are the ones who need to adjust our beliefs to the Word. We should never try to adjust the word of God to accommodate our opinions, or to agree with what some leaders are teaching. The word of God is infallible. We are the ones who need to humble ourselves to understand how things work in the kingdom of God. We need to ask the Lord for more understanding to better serve Him and love Him until Jesus comes back or we go to be with Him.

Chapter 1

TRUE CHURCH VS
SOCIAL CLUB

The assurance of salvation regardless of how you live your life is the central teaching of many churches today. That teaching which is called Once Saved Always Saved (O.S.A.S.), states that salvation cannot be lost once a person receives it. We will see more about this topic in chapter four. To better understand the danger of Once Saved Always Saved, we need to look at how it relates to the sudden-fluffy growth of many churches, and to the increase in suicide among Christians in recent years. I will speak about suicide among believers in chapter six. But by now, I want to call your attention to how that teaching is departing from the Scripture and from what the New Testament church practiced. The believers of the New Testament church had the correct teaching which was reflected in their behaviors; they were not using grace as an excuse for sinning as O.S.A.S. implies. Today, many churches are trying to accommodate the Gospel to please their members to the point of becoming social clubs. A church that conducts itself as a social club may look very appealing, but it will be lacking the essence of the Gospel that makes the difference between being saved or being entertained. Most importantly, a social club could be educating believers for eternal damnation with a doctrine that contradicts the word of God and disregards the need to live holy lives. That kind of teaching is attracting many people, resulting in different mega churches around the world.

Before I go any further, I want to make clear that I truly believe in big congregations. We know that the New Testament church became a mega church in just one day. I also believe that there are mega churches in these days that are serving God according to the Scripture and that are preaching the full Gospel of Jesus Christ. Furthermore, God wants His house to be full because His will is for no one to perish but to have everlasting life.

Mega Church, Little Teaching

However, the Scripture speaks about a new kind of mega church that will arise in the last days. The word of God clearly states the reason why there would be so many of such churches. "For the time will come when they will not endure sound doctrine; but after their own lusts shall they heap to themselves teachers, having itching ears; And they shall turn away their ears from the truth, and shall be turned unto fables" (2 Timothy 4:3-4). As we can see the reason why those churches are spreading so rapidly is because of the character of the believers. Many of these churches are filled with people that gather to hear what they want to hear. They do not want the sound doctrine.

The word of God specifies that this multitude will turn away their ear from the truth. This means that these believers were hearing the truth at some point in their lives, but they found it inconvenient and hard to apply. The Word became a burden for them, thus they turned away from the truth. Those believers prefer to follow their own lusts. Because of that, they gathered for themselves teachers according to their own heart. They looked and found new teachers, preachers, or pastors that are speaking exactly what their itching ears want to hear. And that is the kind of multitude that continues to accumulate in many places. People want to receive a spiritual-fast-food tailored to their own lusts. They want a type of drive-through church that demands no accountability for their actions. They go and get their 'encouraging' sermons and return to their successful lives. They don't even stop for a moment to verify if the doctrine they are receiving is true or not. Those believers give more attention to material food than they give to the spiritual food. They take the time to read the labels, table of nutrition, and calories because they want to make sure that they are receiving the right nutrients for their physical bodies. But the spiritual food is more important to God. Jesus said to those that were following Him only because of the material bread that they should care more for the meal that brings eternal life (John 6:27).

Please notice that there is a combination between false teachers and lustful believers. Many believers are knowingly looking for spiritual leaders and ministers that will support their personal agenda. Similarly, the false prophets are teaching what is not right because of love of money and fame. They turn to fables, little stories, personal opinions, but they are not teaching the word of God.

What about Innocent Christians and False Doctrines

In the middle of this confusion we can find innocent believers who do not know the true Gospel. Those believers come with good intentions and an opened heart; they can easily be impressed by the leaders and deceived by their teaching. I want to emphasize that even when someone is not purposefully looking for wrong doctrine they can lose their soul by listening to false prophets. We learn more about this when Jesus rebuked the Pharisees for recruiting innocent people for their own cause while impeding their salvation. "Woe to you, teachers of the law and Pharisees, you hypocrites! You shut the door of the kingdom of heaven in people's faces. You yourselves do not enter, nor will you let those enter who are trying to" (Matthew 23:13). And if you have any doubt that Jesus was referring to losing salvation and going to hell, let's read a little further: "Woe to you, teachers of the law and Pharisees, you hypocrites! You travel over land and sea to win a single convert, and when you have succeeded, you make them twice as much a child of hell as you are" (Matthew

23:15). Jesus is emphatically saying that someone can go to hell for listening to the wrong doctrine, even if he or she is unaware of it, or has good intentions. We need to pay attention to this truth because it is a matter of eternal death or eternal life.

There Is No Excuse for Not Knowing

We live in a world where people can choose from a variety of churches that will make the gospel more comfortable, attractive and easier to them. But that is not an excuse for not knowing the truth because we also have more Bibles today than ever. It is our responsibility to study the Scripture to verify if what we are listening is in line with the word of God or not. I want to emphasize that one of the main lies being taught today in many churches is that once you are saved you could not lose your salvation even if you sin. Be vigilant to find out what Jesus said about your salvation.

How the New Testament Church Grew

When we look back to the New Testament church, we will find that its growth was caused by the outpouring of Holy Spirit, the teaching of sound doctrine, prayer, and the testimony of transformed believers. The good character of the believers became a witnessing tool to reach the unbelievers. In other words, there was a noticeable difference between Christians and non-Christians in the New Testament church.

The Believer Changed Their Ways After Being Saved

Because of the testimony of the believers, many came to serve the Lord; and the new believers also changed their ways.

They knew that their salvation needed to affect their words and actions. The word of God registers the changes that the believers were experiencing. It was clear that they did not act as if they could behave in any way and still be saved. For example, there were people who got saved who used to practice magic; once they were saved they came forward giving account of their acts, and burning the books of witchcraft in front of the believers. (Acts 18:18-19). Let's continue to see if the change in the way of living of the believers was something casual, or if it was indeed a requirement from God.

When we examine the letters of the apostles to the churches, we will find that the whole purpose of those letters was to change the intentions, the words, and the actions of the believers. Those letters represent a testimony that once we are saved we must change our ways. Let's examine some of those instructions: "But among you there must not be even a hint of sexual immorality, or of any kind of impurity, or of greed, because these are improper for God's holy people. Nor should there be obscenity, foolish talk or coarse joking, which are out of place, but rather thanksgiving. For of this you can be sure: No immoral, impure or greedy person—such a person is an idolater— has any inheritance in the kingdom of Christ and of God" (Ephesians 5:3-5, NIV). The Scripture here is speaking to believers; to people that had been saved. Nevertheless, God is demanding change in their lives. The Scripture here specifies that those who practice evil acts will not inherit the kingdom of God.

Here is another Scripture regarding the need for change in the life of those who have been saved. "If ye then be risen with Christ, seek those things which are above, ...Mortify therefore your members which are upon the earth; fornication, uncleanness, inordinate affection, evil concupiscence, and covetousness, which is idolatry: For which things' sake the wrath of God cometh on the children of disobedience: In the which ye also walked some time, when ye lived in them" (Colossians 3:1-3; 5-9). The Bible continues to name other sins that the believers needed to put away; such as, anger, malice, blasphemy, filthy communication; it also tells us not to lie one to another. Not only that, but the Word tells us about the need to put off the old man with his deeds (Colossians 3:1-3; 5-9). As we can see in this Scripture, Christians are expected to act differently after being saved.

When we were saved we received the ability to obey the word of God; that is the whole purpose of receiving a new nature in Christ. Before being saved we were dead in our sins, but now we have received new life. We can also notice that this Scripture is saying that if we have been risen with Christ our minds shall be set in the things that are above; we are dead—to our old nature— and now our lives are hidden in Christ. But since Christians are not physically dead, what that means is that we must make daily decisions not to please our fleshly desires, and to obey what God says. Our flesh will continue to ask for what is wrong until the day that our bodies are transformed when Jesus returns. Consequently, we need to continue to say no to our desires, and yes to the will of God.

Jesus gave this warning to His disciples, "…except your righteousness shall exceed the righteousness of the scribes and Pharisees, ye shall in no case enter into the kingdom of heaven" (Matthew 5:20). The righteousness of the Pharisees was only of words and appearances. Thus, Jesus is telling the disciples that He expects good deeds and good behavior from them; if not, they should not enter the kingdom of heaven. In the Gospel there is a direct connection between what we believe and what we practice; between what we speak and how we behave. The Gospel is not a mystical religion. The word of God states that in Jesus we were created to do good works (Ephesians 2:10).

Punishment in Grace

The Scripture narrates the work of the Holy Spirit in the New Testament church, not just by working signs and wonders but also by producing holiness in the believers. That fact that holiness was required from the believers is demonstrated with a single act that shocked the newly founded church. I am referring to the sudden death of Ananias and Sapphira. The word of God narrates how Ananias and Sapphira were killed by lying to the Holy Spirit. This was a married couple who sold a land and then pretended to have given the whole price to the apostles. Another brother had brought the whole price of his property, so they simulated to be doing the same. But Peter understood by the Holy Spirit that they had lied regarding the price and confronted the husband who came to bring the offering with these words: "…Ananias, why hath Satan filled thine heart to lie to the Holy Ghost, and to keep back part of the price of the land?" Peter continued to say, "...why hast thou conceived this thing in thine heart? Thou hast not lied unto men, but unto God. And Ananias hearing these words fell down, and gave up the ghost: and great fear came on all them that heard these things" (Acts 5:1-10). Ananias was immediately buried by the young men of the church. After a lapse of about three hours Sapphira his wife also came to the church, and Peter gave her an opportunity to tell the truth. Without knowing what had happened to her husband, she confirmed the same lie that they had agreed upon. Sapphira received the same punishment, and was buried by the same group. (Acts 5:1-10).

As we can see, this judgment from God came during the dispensation of grace, when the church had just begun. This couple was killed as a punishment for lying to the Holy Spirit. As result of this judgment, the believers were not entertaining the idea that they could get away with sin because they were living in the grace. The word of God specified that due to this judgment, the fear of the Lord came upon the believers and the community. I imagine that the young people who had the frightening task of burying this couple had no doubt in their minds that you should not play with God. So, when we see churches growing so fast without being filled with the Holy Spirit, without demonstration of the power of the Spirit, and without the fear of the Lord, we are reading a recipe for heresy. When we take a closer look to what those churches are teaching, we might find that their sudden growth is the product of the leaven that is hidden in their doctrine.

Are My Future Sins Forgiven?

What is the explanation given by those who teach that once you are saved you remain always saved regardless of how you live your life, or what sin you commit? The explanation that they give is that your future sins are already forgiven. The logic of this teaching has no comparison in any legal system or discipline in the world. No system of the world would offer forgiveness of future violations to its laws to anybody. If we observe the nation of Israel for example, whose laws derive from the word of God, they don't forgive future violations to the laws either.

Once Saved Always Saved claims to be based on the word of God, but it completely contradicts the law of God and its application. This teaching has no precedent or logical explanation. There is not even the smallest suggestion in the Bible regarding forgiveness of future sins. That doesn't exist. Let's go to the Scripture: "For if we sin wilfully after that we have received the knowledge of the truth, there remaineth no more sacrifice for sins, but a certain fearful looking for of judgment and fiery indignation, which shall devour the adversaries" (Hebrews 10:26-27). This is Scripture completely contradicts the teaching of forgiveness of future sins; on the contrary, this Scripture is declaring that there is no more sacrifice for those who deliberately sin after being saved. Those believers will experience a great expectation of punishment. However, Once Saved Always Saved has been accepted by many because it makes their lives easy.

Those who want to live their lives doing what they please will blindly embrace that teaching. Eternal assurance and forgiveness of future sins resonates with our modern society that is accustomed to getting things easy and quick. This kind of doctrine seems liberating to the rebel fallen nature that refuses to give account to anyone.

A New Kind of Indulgency

I can compare the teaching of Once Saved Always Saved to the selling of indulgencies made by the traditional church in the middle ages. Indulgencies were part of the system of the Roman Catholic Church that consisted in paying for one's guilt. This system prescribed the use of good works, and even money to pay for the guilt. Indulgencies were pure lies forged by the greediness of leaders to deceive the people and to take away their wealth. To make that falsehood even more lucrative, the church conceived the idea of a purgatory where people would continue to pay for their sins after death. That belief was based on an excessive guilt that persecuted believers all their lives.

Indulgency vs. O.S.A.S.

The Indulgency system and O.S.A.S. are totally wrong; however, I would like to compare, and contrast them to demonstrate the extent of the danger that O.S.A.S. causes in the believers. The similarity between these two beliefs is that both pretend to deal with the ultimate destiny of humans; although, each has a different focus about destiny. For example, Indulgency focused on hell, and gave little attention to heaven—that's why they invented Purgatory. In the other hand, O.S.A.S. emphasizes heaven but does not speak about hell. Another difference between these two teachings is that Indulgencies were purchased by the believers motivated by guilt and fear. Many of those who purchased Indulgencies were sincere believers who were reasonably afraid of hell. Hell is a real geographical place that has a one-way ticket to enter and an irrevocable contract to stay. On the contrary, the believers of O.S.A.S. are buying eternal assurance based on their desire of an easy gospel and independence. The believers of Indulgencies were trying to avoid going to hell; on the other hand, the believers of O.S.A.S. are treating eternal assurance as a token to enter heaven regardless of how they live their lives on this earth. Therefore, the traditional church sold indulgences emphasizing guilt; O.S.A.S. promises eternal security emphasizing freedom from accountability. The former sold terror and fear, the latter sells irrational confidence, carelessness, and defiance. Another area to compare between these doctrines is their attitude toward the sacrifice of Jesus. The practice of Indulgencies completely minimized the power of the sacrifice of Jesus by demanding work and wealth to obtain salvation.

Free, But Not Cheap

Similarly, O.S.A.S. disregards the sacrifice of Jesus by teaching the believers that they don't have to care for their salvation. With an attitude like that O.S.A.S. is treating what is free as it was cheap. Salvation if free for us but it cost Jesus His life!

Another area to examine in these beliefs is their view regarding forgiveness of sins. Because of the greed of the leaders, Indulgencies were designed to never allow for total forgiveness of the believers not even for those who were really repented.

O.S.A.S. however, irrationally assures forgiveness of future sins. By doing so, O.S.A.S. is providing the believers with a license to committing unlimited future sins. As we can see, although the system of Indulgencies was totally wrong, it made more sense than O.S.A.S. because at least Indulgencies pretended to deal with sins that the believers have already committed. O.S.A.S. is not only wrong but is also completely irrational by assuring forgiveness of future sins. As I had mentioned before, this system is illogical because it contradicts everything that the Scripture teaches about the law of God and the responsibility of humans for their actions. Moreover, this belief also despises the value of the blood of Jesus and the Holy Spirit by emphasizing that one can continue to sin after being saved.

We have seen the similarities and differences between two false teachings and their interpretations regarding salvation: the indulgency system of the Catholic Church and Once Saved Always Save, a teaching that is preached by many churches today. Now we want to speak about what is the perfect balance between these two beliefs, because each of these teaching represents a deviation from that truth.

Real Repentance, Real Salvation

You might find this very strange but a belief that regards salvation as something that cannot be lost has one fundamental problem: the person cannot be saved! The reality is that for someone to get saved the individual needs to repent first. And a person cannot repent if he or she thinks that he deserves forgiveness. The attitude of unworthiness is necessary to receive forgiveness. Jesus explained that principle of salvation when he referred to the prayer of the publican and the Pharisee. The Pharisee was speaking about his merits before God, and how good he was, while the publican was at a distance and would not even lift his eyes to heaven for considering himself unworthy of God's forgiveness. Jesus said that the publican was justified. So, a teaching that treats salvation as something that cannot be lost deprives the individual from the feeling of unworthiness that is needed to receive salvation. Many would start taking salvation for granted because they think that they will not lose it regardless of what they do. There is a boastfulness attitude in this kind of belief. We are saved by grace; thus, humbleness is needed to obtain grace. If we have the attitude of 'I have it and that's it', we could fail to meet the condition to receive the grace of God. The word of God is clear when it comes to salvation. God has decided to ignore the sin of the people and has called everyone into repentance (Acts 17:30). So, our cooperation in getting our salvation is to completely repent. We need to recognize that we cannot save ourselves, that we are sinners, and that the judgments of God are fair.

Not Repeating the Same Offense

When we truly repent we cannot start to do the same things that we used to do. Jesus told the adulterous woman, go and sin no more. Jesus is saying the same thing to us through the whole Bible. We need to repent and to change our ways. But If I am still enjoying the bad things that I used to do, if I am still proud about them, I am repented? This is important. The sacrifice of Jesus is perfect; it is not missing anything. However, the condition to receive the sacrifice of Jesus is total repentance. When we are sorry for having done something wrong we will not want to do the same again. The word of God says that whoever hides his sin shall not prosper, but those who confess it and abandon it will find mercy. (Proverbs 28:13). It has been clear since the days of the Old Testament that if we are sorry for our sins we do not commit them again. At least we try with all our heart not to do them again.

Let's go back to the Scripture to consider the life of King David. David committed one of the worst sins that a man can commit, especially a man of God. He committed adultery with the wife of one of his officers and then he sent to kill him to conceal the pregnancy of the woman. This was adultery and murder of an innocent man. Many would use the example of the sin of King David to justify that someone will not lose his salvation by committing a sin. But they may ignore the most important aspect of this story, which is that David repented from all his heart; he cried and confessed without making any excuses for his behavior (Psalms 51 and 32). Most importantly, David did not use his forgiveness as a license to continue to sin. God forgave David because his repentance was genuine. But how do we know that David's repentance was real? David truly repented because never again in his life he committed a similar sin.

That is the difference between the true Gospel of Jesus Christ and the false teachings. Those who taught Indulgencies capitalized on the guilt of the people; while O.S.A.S. capitalizes on the lust and the desire for freedom of the believers. However, the true Gospel of Jesus Christ offers salvation and eternal life to those who truly repent.

There is No Excuse for Being in A False Doctrine Today

When we compare those, who were taught to buy Indulgencies with those who are listening to O.S.A.S. we can find a great difference. The period in which the traditional church introduced the Indulgencies was during the middle Ages. The believers did not have access to Bibles to verify the teachings. The Press had not yet been invented. Thus, they had to depend on what their leaders were telling them. But what about the people who are living in this modern age? We have Bibles in our homes, in our cars, in our electronic devices.

There is no excuse for not knowing what the word of God says. We are responsible for what we are listening. We need to take time to study the word of God to obey it. However, there are many who study the Word to try to justify the lifestyle that they want to live. I firmly believe that because this generation has many means to verify what God has said, we will have a greater accountability before God. Because to the one that more is entrusted, more is demanded. We will not be able to say before God that we did not know what the Bible says. Remember that Jesus was anticipating a greater punishment for the cities that were witnesses of His miracles and did not repent (Matthew 11:21). They had the opportunity to verify the truth, so do we.

TRUE CHURCH VS SOCIAL CLUB

Chapter Summary: False doctrines have provoked sudden and fluffy growth of many churches. There are two classes of Christians participating in those churches: believers that want an easy gospel and believers with good intentions. However, there is no excuse for believing a false doctrine. Today Christians have more Bibles than any other group in history. Consequently, it is our responsibility to study the word of God to obey it. The New Testament church received the whole counsel of the Gospel. The believers were filled with the Holy Spirit, and their lives were transformed so that others could see the difference. The believers were not under the impression that they were free to sin because they were under the grace. They saw judgment in the church and were caring for their salvation with fear and trembling.

O.S.A.S. TRUE OR COUNTERFEIT

Chapter 2

DOCTRINES THAT NEED TO RETURN TO THE CHURCH

Many churches today are picking and choosing from the Word of God. Some are only teaching what they consider to be important for a successful life in this modern age. Before I go any further, let me clarify that many of those teachings are important for a good quality of life. There are, of course, many false doctrines, like the one that is being exposed in this book, which need to be confronted and refuted. But in general, the churches are teaching to the believers how to have a good marriage, how to have good relationships with their family and community, and how to be politer. They are also teaching the believers how to give tithes and offerings, and how to contribute financially to their ministries so that they can help the poor. We can see that Jesus and the Apostles dedicated time to teach those truths to the believers. Those things are good for us and can serve as a testimony of our faith to others; overall, they can help us improve our quality of life on this earth. However, when we study the word of God more deeply we notice that neither Jesus, nor the apostles taught those things on their own. Those teachings are part of the whole counsel of the word of God; and like any other teaching of the Scripture have one final goal: the salvation of our souls. When the church chooses to preach some doctrines and to ignore others, they are raising malnourished believers that will not be able to face and overcome temptations.

O.S.A.S. Is Missing Fundamental Doctrines

When Christians get to the point of considering suicide it is because they had been deprived of fundamental doctrines that were part of the New Testament Church. Let me remind you that the believers of the New Testament church were filled with joy, purpose, and enthusiasm for life, even in the middle of persecution. Why were they so joyful even when they had to endure persecution? They had joy because they knew that there is more to life than what we see in this world. They also knew that they would see Jesus when they died, and that there is reward if we suffer for doing the will of God. Most importantly, the New Testament believers suffered difficulties without ending their lives because they knew that they would be lost forever if they did so.

DOCTRINES THAT NEED TO RETURN TO THE CHURCH

They could know those things because they received all the doctrines of the word of God.

When we compare the early church with today's church we can see a remarkable difference between the two. Many believers today are not being taught that suffering is part of life; particularly, of the Christian life. They don't know that those who want to be faithful to God in this evil system will suffer some form of persecution. "…and all that will live godly in Christ Jesus shall suffer persecution" (2 Timothy 3:12). They are not trained to go through difficult times. So, when they encounter any problem in life, many want to end their own lives. We know that there are many congregations that remain true to the word of God, but there are many others that are not doing so. We need to bring back the whole counsel of the word of God to the church.

We should not be ignoring and rejecting doctrines because we think that they are obsolete. Those same doctrines that seem old and scary, such as the Day of Judgment and hell, are part of the whole counsel of the Word. God has given those instructions to His children so that we can remain focused in eternity, and be motivated to live according to His word. The abandonment of fundamental doctrines in the church has led many believers to look for adventures while disregarding the destiny of their souls. Many forget that the soul is the most valuable thing in life. That is why Jesus came to this world to save that which was lost (Luke 19:10). Jesus marveled at how people did everything to gain the world but at the end lost their souls (Mark 8:36). That did not make sense to Jesus, and should not make sense to us either.

O.S.A.S. TRUE OR COUNTERFEIT

Main Doctrines that Need to Return to the Church

Let's look at some of the main doctrines that have been taken out of the church. They are fundamental teachings of the word of God that the believers need to receive and apply to grow healthily. These are some of those doctrines:

- The Return of Jesus

- Judgment Day

- Hell

- Forgiveness to Be Forgiven by God

- Praying and Fasting

- Study and Meditating on the Word of God

- Rebuking Demons

Looking for the Infilling of the Holy Spirit

- Living a Holy Life

- Witnessing to others and Praying for Jerusalem

If you observe closely you will notice that wherever those truths are not being taught, the believers become discouraged, and lose focus of their eternal destiny and purpose. Moreover, the believers become self-centered, which may be one of the reasons why many entertain suicidal thoughts. So, let's start studying these truths while opening our hearts to receive them.

DOCTRINES THAT NEED TO RETURN TO THE CHURCH

The Return of Jesus

Why do I begin with the teaching of the Return of Jesus? Because I believe that this teaching is the first that needs to return into the church. The goal of the Gospel is to prepare us to meet Jesus to live with Him forever. The expectation for the return of Jesus was so vivid in the early church that the believers would greet each other with the word: *Maranatha*, which means the Lord is coming (1 Corinthians16:22). This fundamental truth has been almost eradicated from many churches.

You might be surprised to know that there are some believers who are completely unaware of the Return of our Lord Jesus Christ. They just don't know that they are supposed to be expecting Jesus to take them out of this world to enjoy His presence, and to reign with Him (Revelation 2:26-27; 20:6). Yet, when we listen to the sermons that many are preaching today, it can be easily understood why they have not heard about this: a lot of preachers are just not talking about it! Please take some time to verify by yourself to be aware and to help others to be aware of the most important event of all time: The Return of our Lord and Savior Jesus Christ. I challenge you to take a closer look at what is being taught today. Most importantly, I encourage you to continue to study your Bible to be more familiar with the instructions that have been given to us so that we can obey them. That day shall not take us by surprise like a thief in the night. We need to remember that the word of God tells us to be prepared. In my book titled, *Faith: Heaven's Currency,* I dedicated a whole chapter (Chap. 10) to refreshing our minds about the Return of

Jesus. The word of God speaks about the sings of the end times, such as war, pestilences, and famine. "…I believe that there is a big problem when we only preach about prosperity, faith to excel, establishing the kingdom on earth, and dominion. It's not that I am against those topics; however, we need to teach about our dual existence. We need to teach the people how to live here on earth, but also how to be ready to see Jesus when He returns, or we die. …". (DeL17 \p 119). But the most dangerous sing of the end time is about the character of the religious people. "That is dangerous because these people operate within the church; they hide under the name of a ministry. They may be pastors, leaders, apostles, deacons, or evangelists. Be careful" (DeL17 \p 122).

Waiting for the Bridegroom

We need to teach and learn about the Coming of Jesus; not just to sound scatological or to be able to debate. We need to remind ourselves and to remind others that we need to be ready. Ignoring the Return of Jesus is like someone taking a trip to another county to marry the love of her life. Nevertheless, on the trip she gets so distracted that she forgets that she is traveling to meet her husband. She loses focus by forgetting the purpose of her trip. And of course, since she forgot that she was getting married, she will not make any special preparations, or buy any special attire, or get any special hair do. My dear reader, that is exactly what is happening to many churches today. Even some churches that are not teaching false doctrines, yet they have forgotten about the wedding day; they have forgotten about our appointment with our Lord Jesus.

DOCTRINES THAT NEED TO RETURN TO THE CHURCH

"Christian Nihilism" – No Purpose

We just have seen that many believers do not know about the return of Jesus for different reasons. However, the worst reason is that many Christians are being told that what they do with their lives doesn't matter because they have been saved and "cannot lose their salvation". So, the believers might be thinking that they don't need to be ready. This is so discouraging. This is like raising children without expecting any good behavior from them. They are not held accountable; nobody cares; is like having two parents but living like an orphan. I imagine that many Christians that are being told those lies may be feeling like orphans; as if no one cares how they behave. It is as if they could do anything and it will not make a difference regarding their salvation. This can result in what my wife calls 'Christian nihilism'. *Nihilism* is the belief that rejects any moral standard and regards life as something meaningless. Unfortunately, some Christians are behaving just like that.

The Christian life as God designed it is rewarding, but it also comes with afflictions. And believe me that there are many afflictions for us as Christians; consequently, the Lord has promised to deliver us from them all (Psalms 34:19). So, when the church stops teaching that Jesus is returning and that we must be ready to meet him, the salt has lost its flavor and life becomes empty. The knowledge and expectation of His coming is what preserves our holiness.

But if Christians are told that they have already received the highest blessing in life without any possibility of losing it, they will live without purpose or goals. As a result, those that are under those lies could experience feelings of emptiness. However, not everyone is going to sit around and feel hopeless; many are setting personal goals that have nothing to do with their spiritual life or with the purpose of God for their lives. They will continue to focus on those goals because they need something to strive for; they need a reason to pursuit excellence. That is how we were created. But when religious leaders tell the believers that they do not need to care for their salvation, they are depriving the believer from their ability to obtain the greatest goal in life, which is the salvation of our soul.

Teachings such as Once Saved Always Saved eliminates the natural sense of accountability for our personal actions given to us by God. Think about it, is this how any system in the world works? Perhaps, you may say, but this is something that comes from God, that is why it is so different from what we know to be normal. Let me remind you that what we know in this life comes from God. The things that are normal and fair come from the laws, statues, and principles that God gave to the people of Israel. Whatever is good also comes from the law that God has written in the heart of every human being. Therefore, God does not deal with humans by trying to deliver them from responsibility for their actions.

Living a Holy Life

DOCTRINES THAT NEED TO RETURN TO THE CHURCH

When Christians understand that they need to be ready for the return of Jesus they will understand the need for holiness. As a result, we will want to shower every day with the water of the word of God to clean off the impurities of our character. Not just to look good before the people but to be ready to see the Holy God; because without holiness we cannot see Him.

There are two areas of holiness. The first part is made by God. The Scripture says that we were separated by God for salvation (Ephesians 1:4). But the other part of holiness is our responsibility. We need to apply the word of God constantly to change our character until it looks like the character of Jesus Who is the image of God. The Scripture says that we are purified by obeying the word of God (1 Peter 1:22). Therefore, our lives need to reflect Who God is. The Apostles were always writing to the believers to remind them how to behave as holy people. God gave us a new nature so that we may be able to obey His word. The Scripture says that without holiness no one will see the Lord. To be able to see the Lord is the purpose of being saved. Remember that salvation is the most important thing in life. God already did His part by calling us, now we need to prepare to see Him.

The Day of Judgment

We need to teach to the people that there is a day that has been appointed by God, where everyone will be before His throne (Hebrews 9:27). This is the most important appointment that we all have. So, why has this teaching been almost completely removed from the church today? By the grace of God, the Scripture also teaches that those who believe in Jesus will not be condemned (John 3:18). To escape giving account for our sins we need to be forgiven by Jesus. Remember that to be forgiven by God we need to truly repent. And when we genuinely repent we make the decision not go back to our old ways. That can take some effort from our behalf, but God expects us to make that effort, for that reason He has given us a new nature by placing His Holy Spirit within us. That new nature helps us overcome the flesh and obey His word. When we choose to obey God's word we are caring for our salvation; God will not do that part for us.

Place Called Hell

When we examine the teachings of Jesus, we find that He always spoke about the terrifying reality of hell, and the lake of fire. In many of His teaching Jesus would mention the place where wailing and gnashing of teeth will happen, where fire will not cease: "But the children of the kingdom shall be cast out into outer darkness: there shall be weeping and gnashing of teeth" (Matthew 8:12). Jesus was constantly mentioning the most dangerous reality that exists. Please look at some of those verses for yourself (Matthew 13:42; 13:50; 22:13; 24:51; 25:30; 25:41).

Jesus included the reality of hell because humans need to know the consequences that they will face if they decide to disobey His word. They also need to know the consequences of despising His sacrifice by not caring for their salvation. We need to teach that to the people. If we don't teach those truths, we are depriving the people from the most precious treasure which is their salvation. Jesus asked what would be the benefit of a person if he wins the whole world and then loses his soul (Mark 8:36). That makes the soul of one single person more valuable than the whole world! Therefore, going to heaven, and escaping hell must be present in every daily decision we make. That is why this teaching needs to return to the church.

Prayer and Fasting

Another teaching that needs to return to the church is regarding prayer and fasting. Jesus gave specific instructions to the disciples on how to pray and fast. (Matthew 6). When we pray and fast, our spirit becomes stronger, and we can be more effective against the demonic powers. We will be ready to advance the Gospel, and God will give us rewards for doing His will.

Rebuking Demons

One of the signs of the believers is to rebuke demons. Jesus explained that to the disciples. He said that in His name we will cast out devils. (Mark 16:17). The church needs to go back to use the power that Jesus has given us. When we start to do that again, many will be delivered from bondage, and the true Gospel will reach multitudes.

Looking for the Infilling of the Holy Spirit

Being filled with the Holy Spirit is a priority for the believer. Jesus told His disciples not to move from Jerusalem until they were filled with the Holy Spirit. We need to bring the power of the Holy Spirit that causes any impure thoughts to flee. The Holy Spirit gives joy to the believers, and cures any anxiety (John 7:37-39). The Holy Spirit also gives power to the believer to preach the Gospel (Acts 1:8).

Witnessing to Others and Praying for Jerusalem

To save ourselves and to save others is the main purpose of the Christian life. We are intercessors before God for the salvation of every person; especially for the people of Israel. We also need to pray for the peace and the restoration of Jerusalem. (Psalms 122:6-9; Isaiah 62). Doing so gives us a purpose that will take attention away from ourselves and from our problems.

Chapter Summary: The Gospel is comprised of many doctrines that need to be taught to the believers. Today, many are disregarding some of those teaching because they consider them obsolete. But those same doctrines that seem old and scary, such as teaching about hell and the Day of Judgment, are part of what makes Christians to remain focused in eternity and holiness. The New Testament church received the whole gospel, for that reason the believers had joy and enthusiasm even in the middle of persecution. Therefore, we need to teach about the Return of Jesus, the infilling of the Holy Spirit, praying and fasting, and everything that Jesus and the disciples taught. When those teachings return to the church, the believers will be strong and will be able to face the difficulties of life.

Chapter 3

WHAT JESUS SAID ABOUT SALVATION

Jesus spoke about salvation, and the different ways in which Christians could lose it. Jesus explained what will be the standard that He will use to determine who will enter heaven and who will be thrown into hell. Remember that Jesus is the One Who knows what the believers need to do to retain the salvation that cost Him His life. Jesus gives salvation the value that it really has because He knows the price that He had to pay for it. Jesus will not tolerate any disrespect to His sacrifice; although He does not want anyone to perish but to have everlasting life. That is the reason why He shed His precious blood for the whole world. Next, we will consider some of the details that Jesus provided that will help us care for our salvation with fear and trembling. I will present those Scriptures in the order in which they appear in the New Testament so that is easier to follow.

It's not Enough to Say, Lord, Lord

Jesus said: "Not everyone that saith unto me, Lord, Lord, shall enter into the kingdom of heaven; but he that doeth the will of my Father which is in heaven. Many will say to me in that day, Lord, Lord, have we not prophesied in thy name? and in thy name have cast out devils? and in thy name done many wonderful works? And then will I profess unto them, I never knew you: depart from me, ye that work iniquity" (Matthew 7:21-23). Jesus is speaking here about Christians; people that had been saved. Jesus is pointing to the fact that those leaders were not doing the will of His Father, and on the contrary, they were doing evil deeds.

Before I go any further, let me explain what iniquity is. Iniquity in the New Testament comes from the word *anomia* referring to being without law. This can be an example of a believer who thinks that he is exempt from obeying the word of God since he has already been saved. Remember that Paul said that he was not without law but under the law of Christ (1 Corinthians 9:21). Jesus expects us to obey the Word. Because we are saved we are expected to do good deeds. We are not saved because of good deeds, but once we are saved we are expected to have good deeds. If Jesus does not find obedience in us He will ask us to depart from Him. Remember on 'that day' those who say Lord, Lord, but do not do good deeds will be asked to depart from Him. (Matthew 7:21-23). Think about this scripture. Jesus is saying that those ministers will tell Him that they had performed miracles in His name. Notice that Jesus does not call them liars for saying that; which means that they were really performing miracles. Instead, Jesus rebuked them for their lawlessness. In other words, their miracles were fine, but their behaviors were wrong. Their ways did not reflect the will of the Father; so, they will be asked to depart from Him.

If It Impedes You Cut It Off

Another scripture where Jesus speaks about salvation says: "Woe unto the world because of offenses! for it must needs be that of fences come; but woe to that man by whom the offense cometh! Wherefore if thy hand or thy foot offend thee, cut them off, and cast them from thee: it is better for thee to enter into life halt or maimed, rather than having two hands or two feet to be cast into everlasting fire. And if thine eye offend thee, pluck it out, and cast it from thee: it is better for thee to enter into life with one eye, rather than having two eyes to be cast into hell fire" (Matthew 18:6-9). To begin analyzing this scripture, please notice the graphic language that Jesus is using here. Jesus is speaking about plucking out eyes and cutting off limbs; although Christians have never interpreted these verses as a call for mutilation, Jesus' phrasing highlights the important of escaping hell. Escaping hell is the greatest goal of our Christian life. Jesus always put this priority at the top of His teachings. So, let's look at this Scripture a little closer. Here Jesus is speaking to people that are saved. He is saying to them that if one of their eyes is going to cause them to go to hell, then it is better to pluck it out and enter eternal life with one eye than to have both eyes and be cast into hell. This is the reality of salvation. Jesus never took salvation lightly. Salvation has to do with the place where will spend eternity!

Only God can save us, but only we can abandon the things that threaten our salvation and can lead us to perdition. We needed to be rescued by God from our sins, and spiritual death, but once we have been rescued we need to do our part to remain saved. If we did not have to look after our salvation, what would be the meaning of a teaching like that? Why would Jesus instruct the believers to take such drastic measures, if necessary, to preserve their salvation? Today many are treating salvation carelessly. Remember that salvation cost Jesus His life. We could not have paid for our salvation, but we should appreciate it by care for it with fear and trembling; that is our responsibility. Jesus will not do that part for us. In this Scripture, Jesus is clearly teaching that we could perish if we do not remove from our lives whatever presents a threat to our salvation.

It Is Wise to Be Ready

There is another scripture where Jesus speaks about how to preserve our salvation. This scripture is found in Matthew, chapter 25. Here Jesus speaks about ten virgins getting ready to meet a groom to celebrate a wedding. I think that it is fair to say that these ten virgins were all saved. They all had oil in their lamps. But while they all fell asleep, there was one big difference between the two groups. The five wise virgins were prepared and ready to follow the groom when he arrived; but the five foolish virgins did not prepare their lamps with enough oil to receive the groom. We could say that they did not do what was needed to remain saved so that they could enter the wedding. At the end Jesus said these words: "And while they went to buy, the bridegroom came; and they that were ready went in with him to the marriage: and the door was shut. Afterward came also the other virgins, saying, Lord, Lord, open to us. But he answered and said, Verily I say unto you, I know you not. Watch therefore, for ye know neither the day nor the hour wherein the Son of man cometh" (Matthew 25:10-13). As we can see, it does make a difference what we do after we have been saved.

No Dress, No Dinner

Let us see another example. Jesus gave another parable to make the disciples aware of their responsibility to be ready to meet Him. In this Scripture Jesus is speaking about a king that invited many people to His banquet. Some rejected the invitation by giving excuses; others even killed those that brought them because they did not appreciate the king's invitation. Nevertheless, the king persisted in having his celebration and sent his servants to bring whoever they found. So, the servants went to the streets and to the roads and brought all kinds of people and the wedding room was filled. And this is what happened. "…But when the king came in to see the guests, he noticed a man there who was not wearing wedding clothes. He asked, 'How did you get in here without wedding clothes, friend?' The man was speechless. Then the king told the attendants, 'Tie him hand and foot, and throw him outside, into the darkness, where there will be weeping and gnashing of teeth" (Matthew 22:11-13, NIV). As we can see, this scripture is referring to salvation. Why? Because Jesus clearly states that the man was cast into the darkness where there will be weeping and gnashing of teeth. Jesus uses this expression when speaking about hell in other scriptures. What do we see here? In here we had an open invitation to a wedding, and it was free. But there was one condition; everyone needed to put on a wedding garment before entering the feast. It seems very apparent that the garment was also provided to the guests because the man had no excuse to give to the king for not being properly dressed. He just did not feel like wearing the special garment. He was so lazy that he did not want to change and to put on new clothing; he wanted to stay in his comfort zone. He just went into the wedding with his same old ways, same old character, and same old behavior. The king commanded him to be cast out to the darkness without thinking it twice.

Who Is Called and Who Is Chosen

At the end of the parable of the wedding and the guest that was not properly dressed, Jesus said something that is not part of the parable (Matthew 22:11-14). Jesus gave a principle to explain what happened at the banquet; He said: 'many are called and few are chosen.' This is a choice, but whose choice is it. Many people would use this Scripture as a foundation for the theology of predestination. Nevertheless, we should take time to try to understand what Jesus was really declaring. What does it mean to be chosen? We can notice that the rest of the guests were both called and were dressed accordingly; that is why they were not cast away. What makes the difference between being called and being chosen? The difference is in the preparation. You can be called to attend the wedding, but it is your choice to wear or not to wear the wedding garment. The man that was not dressed in the wedding apparel despised the occasion. He thought that since the invitation was free, why bother to dress in any specific way. He did not appreciate the occasion or the presence of the king. He assumed that if the king was so desperate to have his house filled with guests, then he would have to tolerate whatever the guests wanted to wear. But he was wrong.

Jesus is giving this parable to teach us the great reality of salvation. We are called to take off the old dress of our bad actions and to put on the new dress of the fruit of the Spirit "...put off all these; anger, wrath, malice, blasphemy, filthy communication out of your mouth. Lie not one to another, seeing that ye have put off the old man with his deeds; And have put on the new man, which is renewed in knowledge after the image of him that created him" (Colossians 3:8-10). Making changes in the way that we speak, and act is what constitutes the wedding dress that we must wear as Christians. The scripture says regarding the dress of the bride of the Lamb, that the white line that she is wearing is the good deeds of the saints. (Revelation 19:8). We shall not be boasting or making excuses for remaining in sin. Jesus made it very clear that those who do not make changes in their ways of living after they are saved will not enter His kingdom. Jesus taught about that subject both, in parables and in direct teaching to the believers. Furthermore, the word of God denounces the temptation of remaining in sin after being saved with the following questions: "…Shall we continue in sin, that grace may abound?" God forbid. How shall we, that are dead to sin, live any longer therein" (Romans 6:1-2). So, it is very clear that good works shall follow salvation.

Chapter Summary: By studying some of the teachings of Jesus regarding Salvation we found the following truths:

- Those who perform miracles but also live in iniquity will have to depart from Jesus.

- We need to get rid of anything that is a temptation to us to protect our salvation.

- We need to be fully equipped with oil in our lamps for us to enter with the bridegroom to the wedding.

- We need to be dressed in holiness to enter the wedding because many are called, and few are chosen.

- The chosen ones are those who get ready. The man in the parable of the wedding did not have any excuse for not being ready, and was cast out into the darkness.

Chapter 4

O.S.A.S. - Truth or Counterfeit

In the first chapter we have seen a definition of Once Saved Always Saved and its relation to the true church and the social club. This doctrine is based on John Calvin's interpretation of the words that Jesus spoke regarding how only God can draw sinners to Him (John 6:44). That Scripture indicated to Calvin that when God selects someone for salvation the individual will remain saved regardless of what they do after being saved. One of the problems with this doctrine is that many are using it as a license to sin. We understand by looking to the whole counsel of the word of God that this doctrine does not represents how God deals with humans, and does not relate to how humans were created to function. In this chapter I want to present biblical proof for why this teaching is a trap of eternal consequences for the believers, and why we need to be able to expose it and refute it.

If we look around us we will see that wherever there is a truth, a falsehood appears to contradict it. So, it is very important to be able to distinguish between the two. Where does the counterfeit come from? The word of God speaks about how the enemy sowed a counterfeit seed in the field of the Lord (Matthew 13:24-30). The enemy is who infiltrates false teachings using false teachers to deceive the people of God. Jesus spoke a parable to teach us this truth. From this parable we can understand a reality about counterfeit: the enemy does not need to use a counterfeit to deceive people who are openly serving him. He does that in the church to disguise his lies under a religious cover. Therefore, the worst damage can be done from within. We are responsible for becoming experts at distinguishing between the true doctrine and the counterfeit.

Building with Cheap Materials

There is a common practice among those who falsify a product. They remove a good ingredient from the product and substitute it with another ingredient of inferior quality. In summary, they do that because it costs them less to make that product and gives them more revenue. That is why some pastors and spiritual leaders are substituting the pure ingredients of the word of God with philosophy, personal opinions, and practices that have nothing to do with the goal of the Gospel.

O.S.A.S. TRUE OR COUNTERFEIT

Those religious leaders are teaching contaminated doctrines because it makes their job easier, they save time, and make a lot of money! But we need to think from the perspective of the consumer of that product. Would you continue to buy a product that you know has been altered? Would you continue to buy it even when you know that it will affect your health? Would you use it just to save a few dollars? Now, look all the previously asked questions and let's assume that you answered yes to all of them; meaning that you will use the falsified product. What about if instead of costing you less, you would have to pay double, would you still buy it? Now imagine that instead of dealing with material products that can affect your physical body you were dealing with spiritual food that would affect your soul for eternity.

Many are treating spiritual matters like a falsifier would treat a material product; taking ingredients in and out at their discretion motivated by covetousness. The word of God says, "And through covetousness shall they with feigned words make merchandise of you..." (2 Peter 2:3). Let me give you that same Scripture in another version: "In their greed these teachers will exploit you with fabricated stories..." (2 Peter 2:3, NIV). Moreover, the word of God states that many are building in the gospel with cheap materials. But the Lord will test their works with fire (1 Corinthians 3:13). Cheap material can look very good until a fire breaks out and burns down the materials that are not original. My dear brother or sister, the Lord knew that this was going to happen and gave us this warning. We need to go back and teach the pure and unadulterated Gospel of Jesus Christ.

O.S.A.S. TRUE OR COUNTERFEIT

Four Areas Affected by O.S.A.S.

Any teaching that departs from the truth is a quick road to perdition. To better understand the deceitfulness of Once Saved Always Saved, we need to look at four areas in which this teaching can affect the believers, making them vulnerable to destruction. The four areas affected by this teaching are the following:

Number one, the teaching of O.S.A.S. interferes with the pursuit of excellence intrinsic to human nature. The word of God says that the path of the just is like the morning sun that shines and shines until the day is perfect (Proverbs 4:18, NIV). When the believers are told that there is nothing required from them once they are saved, they are left with little to no desire of pursuing excellence in their spiritual lives. The purpose of holiness is for the believers to be able to look more like their Heavenly Father every day. Holiness is possible, that is why God demands it. Holiness can only be manifested in the lives of those that have received a new nature.

There is also another reason why humans need to overcome and pursuit excellence. That need for challenges helps us fight the nature of decay that came to humans from the disobedience that took place in the Garden of Eden. As a result, if we are not getting better, we are getting worse; if we are not regenerating, we are degenerating. If we are not renewing our minds, we are conforming to the world. If we are not guarding our behavior we are deviating from what is right. Most importantly, if we are not caring for our salvation, we will be living careless lives that could lead us to eternal damnation. This is an undeniable truth.

Number two, O.S.A.S. affects the past, the present, and the future of the person that follows that teaching. This teaching does not draw a clear line to separate the past, the present, and the future condition of our sins. How does this happen? It happens by emphasizing that once you receive your salvation, whatever you do at the present will not affect your future because your future sins were already forgiven in the past. In practice what that teaching implies is that salvation is something that you deserve. Thus, when you finally get it you don't really have to pay any attention to it because you cannot lose it! As a result, the believers do not have appreciation for the way that they were pulled out of their sinful past; they cannot appreciate where they are now, and where they will be. With this nothing-makes-a-difference attitude! the believer is trained to take his salvation for granted or to even disdain it. Why care for something that will be there regardless? Why bother maintaining a holy lifestyle if whatever you do will yield the same results and take you to the same destiny.

Once Saved Always Saved leaves the believers without any goal, or sense of direction. That lack of direction is what causes many Christians to feel hopeless, looking for ways to fill a void that can only be filled with the Spirit of God. The believer can become indifferent to the word of God; and instead, they find other things to focus fully on. Consequently, many are giving all their attention to their pets, cars, electronic devices, houses, clothing, and businesses. They are caring for their material possessions with 'fear and trembling' because they are convinced that their salvation and their relationship with God does not deserve or demand such attention.

Number three: O.S.A.S. can affect every relationship in the lives of the believers. It does this by releasing the individual of moral responsibility for their actions that is necessary in any healthy relationship. For example, this type of teaching will not lay the foundation to maintain faithfulness between a husband and a wife. Think about this. If a believer is tempted to commit an infidelity, and he or she has been trained to believe that what they are about to commit has been already forgiven, it would be easier to fall in such temptation. The devil would use that same teaching to convince the believer to sin. Why worry about it? Why to avoid it? If it happens, it happens'. The same reality applies to any other relationship that requires loyalty and honesty. When the standard allows anything, it becomes a legal license to sin.

God's Reward System

O.S.A.S not only interferes with how humans were created to function, but it also interferes with God's reward system. God has designed a whole system that relies on His character. God is Love, and He is also a Rewarder; He loves to reward humans. For this reason, God created us with a desire for rewards embed in our souls that move us to overcome, to strive, and to become better. Therefore, any teaching that ignores this reality is destined to cause an unbalance in the way that humans think, feel, and behave. Accordingly, to tell the believers that they don't need to make any effort to remain in possession of their salvation is an assault on the very essence of what drives them. Consequently, when people do not think that there is any requirement from them, we are disrupting God's reward system.

Natural Challenges

Now let's look at how a teaching that does not require you to meet any specific standard could be applied in a work place, for example. Imagine that you get a job. And after being hired your manager tells you that once you are hired there is nothing that you can do that will make you lose your job. So, you could come in late, leave early, waste time, or misbehave and still not lose your job. I would like to ask you; would you be happy in such a job? I would assume that you would enjoy it for some time. But after a while you will be bored and even feel bad for not having any standard to meet; and for not producing anything, and for not making any contribution to the company. Why is that? because humans were designed by God to be fruitful, to multiply, and to conquer. We were created with a built-in moral standard that comes from the image of God that we all bear.

If we are in a place where we are permitted to do whatever we want, we might enjoy it for a while but in the long run, emptiness, desperation, and even depression is going to come into our lives. We need to remember that the word of God frequently speaks about salvation as something that will be manifested (1 Peter 1:5). The Scripture said that the goal of our faith is the salvation of our souls (1 Peter 1:9). A goal is something that has been set to be reached. Accordingly, when you have a goal you stay focused and motivated to do what God has said that you should do. The word of God also says that we must work out our salvation with fear and trembling (Philippians 2:12). Those things are part of what makes life meaningful and exciting regardless of our trials and tribulations.

Obedience Was Required Before the Fall

Some may think that Christians should not have the stress of having to care for their salvation. But what does the word of teach? Let's go to the beginning, even before any sin was committed. Let's look at Adam and Eve in the Garden. God gave them everything that they could ever want or need. God declared them the rulers of every living thing. Moreover, God made provision for their dominion to be increased until it would reach the whole world. But even in this rich environment and under that perfect human state, God gave Adam and Eve a commandment to obey, and explained the consequences of disobedience. He told them what to do, what not to do, and the results of their choice. This is a principle that must be applied when we are giving instructions to someone.

Humans need to know what is expected from them, what is prohibited for them, and what will happen if they do not follow the rules. Consequently, God told Adam and Eve that they could eat from every tree, and told them from what tree they should not eat. God also clearly explained to them the consequences that they would face if they decided to eat from the forbidden tree: they should certainly die. What do you notice here my dear reader? God was giving authority to mankind, but He was also setting rules. Why? Because every being created by God has free will. But free will cannot be exercised without having the option to obey or to disobey God's rules.

O.S.A.S. TRUE OR COUNTERFEIT

Rules Are a Highway to Promotion

Another reason for establishing rules is because in God's system every time that we choose what is right we get promoted to a higher level. And every time that we choose what is wrong we face the consequences of our decisions. The reason why God wants to promote us is because He is the Rewarder of those who seek Him. God wants to lift us up because He is the Most High. On the contrary, the devil tempts humans to break God's law. He wants us to fall because he is fallen; he has been eating dust for a long time. "So, the Lord God said to the serpent, …Cursed are you above all livestock and all wild animals! You will crawl on your belly and you will eat dust all the days of your life" (Genesis 3:14). Thus, the enemy is low and wants to bring us down. But God continues to reward us, not just by obeying His word but also for rejecting the lies and temptations of the enemy. God uses those occasions to pull us up even higher so that we can be motivated to overcome.

The Real Agenda of Once Saved Always Saved

Number four. O.S.A.S. views suicide as an alternative. The believer is taught that there are no consequences for committing suicide. The believer is assured that he or she would only loose rewards, but not salvation. And of course, this is the most dangerous part of this doctrine. I speak in more detail about this subject in chapter 6. I invite you to study the evidence of the word of God so that you can avoid falling in such a trap, and can prevent others from falling in the same trap.

Free Will and Predestination

Now let's consider the role of free will regarding salvation. Together with the teaching of once saved always saved is the theology of predestination. Although this is a very complicated issue, I would like to briefly consider some aspects about predestination. According to those under this belief, God has preordained who is going to be saved and who is going to be lost. Based on this belief, once a person is saved there is nothing that he or she can do to lose their salvation, because they did nothing to earn it. They also teach that you don't need to do anything to retain your salvation. The person can live any type of life that he deems appropriate and still be able to see the Lord. They teach that the only thing that can be affected would be the amount of reward that the believers will receive when they get to heaven.

When you look deeper into that teaching, there are a few questions that need to be asked. If a person cannot avoid sinning, would it be fair for God to punish them for doing what they are unable to avoid? If a person cannot obtain salvation because she has not been elected by God for salvation, would it be fair for God to send her to hell? When we consider these questions, we must recognize that something does not match with that theology. The Scripture teaches that God will send the lost to hell; the scripture also reveals that God is just.

One of the greatest proofs to the idea that we can decide to change after we are saved comes from answering the following question. If there was nothing that we could do after being saved, why is there is so much emphasis in the word of God regarding the importance of living godly lives?

O.S.A.S. TRUE OR COUNTERFEIT

The word of God clearly tells us that what we do can make a difference in our destiny. Let's consider the following Scripture: "For if we sin willfully after that we have received the knowledge of the truth, there remaineth no more sacrifice for sins, But a certain fearful looking for of judgment and fiery indignation, which shall devour the adversaries" (Hebrews 10:26-27). This Scripture contradicts those who teach predestination, and those who insist salvation cannot be lost. Furthermore, this Scripture is clearly saying that Christians can decide to turn back from the faith after being saved and sanctified.

Think about this: God did not create robots; He created human beings with the freedom to decide. As a result, when we try to eliminate free will from the teaching of the Gospel we are unleashing spiritual lawlessness and moral chaos. This teaching is totally contrary to the way in which God has related with humans since the beginning. Remember that when God placed Adam and Eve in the garden He treated them as beings that were created in His image, who have the capacity of making decisions regarding their own destiny. God gave them instructions, choices, and explained the consequences of their decisions. Likewise, throughout the Scripture we find the believers using their free will. For example, Apostle Paul described his own struggles in making the right choice: "But I keep under my body, and bring it into subjection: lest that by any means, when I have preached to others, I myself should be a castaway" (1 Corinthians 9:27). Here we see Paul fighting against his own body, his own sinful and rebellious nature; that nature that combats us. Paul made the decision to fight to retain the very same gift of salvation that he had preached to others.

Therefore, it is evident that we can make the decision with our free will to do what is necessary to retain our salvation. Apostle Paul was doing just that. To teach that there is nothing that a person can do that would make her lose salvation is like saying that the believers were programmed for salvation. And if you are programed, then you are a robot, not a human being. God did not create robots; He created free-willed beings. When believers treat salvation as something that cannot be lost, they could take it as something unworthy of appreciation.

Consequences of Sinning Willingly

O.S.A.S. is a dangerous teaching that will bring the punishment of God upon the people that practice it and a stronger judgment upon those who teach it. Those that teach once saved always saved are training the believers to overlook the sacrifice that Jesus made on the cross, to treat the blood of the covenant as meaningless, and to despise the Spirit of grace (Hebrews 10:29). God takes revenge on those who disrespect the sacrifice of Jesus and despise the Holy Spirit. "For we know him that hath said, Vengeance belongeth unto me, I will recompense, saith the Lord. And again, The Lord shall judge his people. It is a fearful thing to fall into the hands of the living God" (Hebrews 10:30-31). This is a serious warning my friend. That warning was given to believers that were living in the grace of God. Those believers had been washed with the precious blood of Jesus and were sanctified.

Nevertheless, they could lose their salvation by sinning persistently and deliberately.

The word of God says, "He that despised Moses' law died without mercy under two or three witnesses" (Hebrews 10:28). And the Scripture asks how much severe punishment should receive the person who despairs the sacrifice of Jesus (Hebrews 10:28-29). In this Scripture we can clearly see that God is referring to those who after being saved have returned to a life of sin. The Scripture continues to explain the consequences of such an act: "For if we sin willfully after that we have received the knowledge of the truth, there remaineth no more sacrifice for sins, But a certain fearful looking for of judgment and fiery indignation, which shall devour the adversaries" (Hebrews 10:26-27). So, if we take salvation for granted we will be severely punished by God, and there will be no more forgiveness for future sins. That is what the word of God is saying.

Let's Us Defend Our Faith

Instead of teaching false doctrines what we need to do is to stand firm in our faith. That does not mean to physically fight or to personally attack anyone; nevertheless, we need to have the boldness to give to others the reasons that make us believe what we believe. When we do that we are giving others an opportunity to be convinced by the Holy Spirit about salvation. But we must do this with love, meekness, and respect (1 Peter 3:15). My dear reader, you cannot please everyone unless you want to perish eternally with them. We need to stop dancing with the devil while pretending to be hugging God.

Jesus said that no one can serve two masters because they will have to decide to please one and to despise the other. Jesus ended this warning saying "Ye cannot serve God and mammon" (Matthew 6:24). Many people believe that Jesus was just referring to money. But it seems that Jesus was also referring to the worldly system that intends to live without God. People that claim to be self-sufficient and because of that they do not have the Lord in their plans. We need to understand that we cannot serve God and the world system which also includes the love of money. What happens when this world system becomes part of the agenda of many leaders. There are those who are compromising the message of the Gospel because of wealth.

We cannot serve God and the world. The world offers fame to those who are willing to alter the message of Jesus. We need to be determined in our minds to please God first. If we want to please the world, we will not please Jesus. But if we decide to preach the message in the way that God intended it to be preached, then we are going to suffer persecution. Nevertheless, the word of God says that this world will pass away with its lust but those who do the will of God will remain forever (1 John 2:17). We need to get up and defend the word of God with our testimony and with our words. By doing so we will rescue those who are about to be lost forever.

Chapter Summary:

- Salvation is something that must be preserved throughout the life of a believer.

- God made humans, not robots. He wanted us to come to Him with our will. God does not force us to follow His Commandments. Nevertheless, they will be consequences if we decide to disobey. Accordingly, we should choose to follow Him, and obey what He said.

- Once saved always saved is a dangerous doctrine that tries to free us of all moral responsibility, and can affect every aspect of our lives and relationships.

- Those that preach this kind of ideology will be punished, alongside those that practice it.

- Salvation is free, not because it is cheap, but because we would never be able to afford it. Therefore, we should cherish the sacrifice that Christ made for us by living a life of holiness, in gratitude for His invaluable sacrifice. Keeping in mind that through disobedience and ingratitude we are at risk of spending an eternity in hell.

Chapter 5

IDENTIFYING AND ABANDONING SIN

Two Choices: Holiness or Sin

Some of the truths of the Scripture are hard to even express; however, we need to speak about them to defeat our sinful nature to be able to please our Lord. If I don't tell you about these truths, then I will be another person educating people to perish like hundreds are doing today. Many today are not interested in speaking the truth of the Gospel of Jesus Christ; instead they are focused on their personal agenda. There is one and determinant truth in the Gospel: we need to save our souls. There are only two options in Christian life: holiness or sin. And there are only two places where we can go after we leave this world: heaven or hell. If we choose to live in holiness we will see the Lord, but if we decide to live ungodly lives hell is the only place where we will go. There is not such a thing as just losing rewards for living in sin. Do not be deceived, wrong communication corrupts good behavior (1 Corinthians 15:33). Free yourself from condemnation.

There are many types of sins that can prevent us eternally from enjoying the presence of God if they do not repent, and abandon them immediately. I invite you to take some time to verify these truths on your own. May the Holy Spirit enlighten your understanding and touch your heart so that you can maintain a life of faithfulness to God.

The word of God says that he that commits sin is of the devil because the devil sinned from the beginning. Those who continue to live in sin are imitating the evil one; and by doing so they are saying that they belong to him. But the word of God goes beyond just identifying the problem; it also gives us the solution to the problem. Thus, the word declares that Jesus came to destroy the works of the devil. (1 John 3:8). And Jesus has also given us authority over all the powers of the enemy and nothing can harm us (Luke 10:19). But to be able to exercise our authority over the enemy we shall not be doing his works. Instead, we shall be living in holiness in all our manners of conversation because God has called us to be holy because He is holy "...Be ye holy, for I am holy" (1 Peter 1:15-17). God will not accept any sin in His presence. The children tend to be like their parents; as sons and daughters of God we shall be holy because our Father is holy.

IDENTIFYING AND ABANDONING SIN

The word of God is what sanctifies us (John 17:17). Our Heavenly Father has given us His word and His Holy Spirit to helps us to obey His word.

What Is Sin?

God describes sin as the violation or transgression of His laws. "Whosoever committeth sin transgresseth also the law: for sin is the transgression of the law" (1John 3:4). God has given us good things and good laws which are for our benefit when we obey them. God gave good and easy laws to Adam and Eve. Those instructions were for their promotion; however, Adam and Eve chose to disobey God. What was the byproduct of their disobedience? It was death; physical death and spiritual death. Adam and Eve got in trouble along with the whole human race. God also gave good laws to the people of Israel, but they disobeyed many times and were punished repeatedly. The Scripture says that all injustice is sin, and the unrighteous shall not inherit the kingdom of God. Furthermore, the word of God provides a list of sins that can prevent a person from inheriting the kingdom of God: "Know ye not that the unrighteous shall not inherit the kingdom of God? Be not deceived: neither fornicators, nor idolaters, nor adulterers, nor effeminate, nor abusers of themselves with mankind…" (1 Corinthians 6:9).

List of Sins that Can Send Christians to Hell

Let's take a closer look at the sins that can prevent a Christian from entering heaven:

Idolatry: idolatry is to have something or someone in first place in your heart. The first place belongs only to God. Watch out, because many people are idolaters without even knowing it. For example, if your son or your daughter gets the most attention from you, then they are your god; it could be your job, your car; pleasures, or entertainment. Any worship given to anyone besides the God of Israel is received by demons, and that person will hate you, no matter what you do to please that individual. He or she will reject you. That is why we see so many wives being hated by their husbands, husbands being hated by their wives, mothers, fathers, family members that are good people being hated by their loved ones. They will try to do whatever it takes to make their love ones happy, but they end up being hated instead. Why? They are worshiping people and not God, which is the Creator of heaven and earth.

You should not be making any material thing the source of your security or to give the ultimate allegiance to any created thing or being. Idolatry, therefore will take people to hell. Only Jehovah is God, there is no other God. (Isaiah 45:18). God clearly states that we shall not have other gods; He warned His people against worshiping the sun, the moon, the hosts of heaven, and any other being or item in the universe. (Exodus 20:3). God also required that the gentile who had believed in the Gospel to stay away from idolatry. "As for the Gentile believers, we have written to them our decision that they should abstain from food sacrificed to idols, from blood, from the meat of strangled animals and from sexual immorality" (Acts 21:25). The word of God also commands the believer not to keep company, or even to eat with those who call themselves Christians but continue to practice idolatry and other sins. "But now I have written unto you not to keep company, if any man that is called a brother be a fornicator, or covetous, or an idolater, or a railer, or a drunkard, or an extortioner; with such an one no not to eat" (1 Corinthians 5:11). Moreover, the Scripture states that there is no agreement between the temple of God and idols (2 Corinthians 6:16). One of the most direct warnings against idolatry in the New Testament simply states: "Little children, keep yourselves from idols. Amen" (1 John 5:21).

My dear friend if you are reading this book and are thinking in your heart that a good God will never send people to hell, let me remind you that God has given everyone the road to follow and we must follow it. But God will not change what is written, He is the same today, yesterday, and forever. He will never change His word to accommodate anyone not even for Himself. Idolatry will take people to perdition. Let's be careful people of God.

Fornication is any type of sexual relation that is not between a husband and wife, a man and a woman who are married. Fornication includes sex with children or pederasty, homosexuality, sex with animals, and any other sexual practice or sexual relationship that is contrary to what God has established. This includes sexual intercourse before marriage. Even more, any adultery is also fornication. Adultery and fornication can also refer to spiritual unfaithfulness to God. Furthermore, most divorces qualify as fornication and adultery under God's standards. "And I say unto you, whosoever shall put away his wife, except it be for fornication, and shall marry another, committeth adultery: and whoso marrieth her who is put away doth commit adultery" (Matthew 19:9). Many ask questions like what shall I do if I got remarried after divorcing my previous spouse for a reason other than adultery? I believe that as with any other sin that we have committed the solution is to repent. That doesn't mean that you must divorce the person to whom you are married now, but you can repent. You should recognize that you have broken God's Law and wholeheartedly repent. Acknowledge your sin before Him and do not divorce again. Fight for the marriage that you now have. Remember that when we are really repented we do not commit the same sin again.

You may ask what about domestic violence as a reason for divorce. I firmly believe that domestic violence is another reason for divorce to be permitted by God. The word of God does not mention domestic violence in the Law of Moses as one of the reasons for divorce because there seemed to be no violence in the marriage in Israel. I want to give my opinion regarding the fact that Moses allowed the men to divorce their wives for anything. Jesus explained that Moses did that because of the hardness of their hearts. It may look as if divorce in such cases was intended to avoid any type violence in the marriage. I believe that God preferred to tolerate divorce rather than seeing one of His precious daughters being mistreated by their husbands.

Murder: this sin includes premeditation, malice, and intentional killing of another human life. The word of God is clear: "Thou shall not kill" (Exodus 20:18). Jesus said that the devil was a murderer since the beginning (Jn. 8:44). For Christians this sin seems as a remote possibility. However, when we take a closer look to how God considers murder we might be surprised. We could find that we are murderers even without knowing it. Please read this Scripture carefully: "Whosoever hateth his brother is a murderer: and ye know that no murderer hath eternal life abiding in him" (1 John 3:15). Under this definition someone who calls himself a Christian can be a murderer before God by hating his brother or sister. And the implications of being a murderer are very well explained by God in this verse: …no murderer has eternal life in Him. And if we don't have eternal life, then we have eternal damnation because there are only two places where we can spend eternity.

Blasphemy against the Holy Spirit: Blasphemy is to attribute the work of God to the devil. This type of sin can be committed by those that have real knowledge about the truth but decide to deny it because of personal interests. In the Bible we find that the Pharisees committed this sin. After Jesus rebuked a demon that was dumb from a man, the Pharisees said that Jesus was rebuking devils by Beelzebub. (Luke 11:14-15). The word of God is clear regarding this type of sin, both in the Old and New the Testaments: And he that blasphemeth the name of the Lord, he shall surely be put to death…" (Leviticus 24:16). The Lord Jesus spoke regarding blasphemy with all authority saying: "Wherefore

I say unto you, all manner of sin and blasphemy shall be forgiven unto men: but the blasphemy against the Holy Ghost shall not be forgiven unto men. Then Jesus took time to emphasize that whoever speaks a word against the Son of man, it shall be forgiven to him but whoever speaks against the Holy Spirit, it shall not be forgiven to him, neither in this world neither in the world to come. (Matthew 12:31-31). Pay attention to this warning this type of sin shall never be forgiven. We need to give the glory to God for what He has done in our lives, and not to attribute His miracles to anybody else.

Adultery: is a violation of the institution of marriage. God said: "Thou shalt not commit adultery" (Exodus 20:14). God sees the covenant of marriage as a covenant with Him. Speaking regarding a woman who commits adultery the word says: "who has left the partner of her youth and ignored the covenant she made before God" (Proverbs 2:17). Moreover, Jesus explained to the people that adultery can take place even in the heart. "But I tell you that anyone who looks at a woman lustfully has already committed adultery with her in his heart" (Matthew 5:28). The heart is the place where our thoughts, emotions, and will reside. And from within the heart of the people comes out all kinds of sin such as evil thoughts, adulteries, fornications, and murders. (Mark 7:21). Therefore, an extramarital sexual relation can happen both in heart and in actions; that includes immoral thoughts and lusting by pornography.

Lasciviousness: is a sin that includes a disorderly desire for sex, pleasure, money, food, drugs, alcohol, and more. A lascivious person is a captive of lust; therefore, he or she is constantly thinking of satisfying their lust; but lust can never be satisfied; it is like a thirst that cannot be quenched. As a result, lust will consume all the energy, time, and resources of the person who is under that self-imposed trap. The word of God declares that people surrender to those desires, "Who being past feeling have given themselves over unto lasciviousness, to work all uncleanness with greediness" (Ephesians 4:19). Lasciviousness is part of the work of the flesh together with adultery, fornication, and uncleanness (Galatians 5:19). What does the scripture mean when it says that something is the work of the flesh? It means that we have the power to stop it and abandon it. God has given us His Spirit to live inside of us so that we can overcome any of our fleshly desires. As Christians we must leave those unholy desires in the past. As the Word says, "For you have spent enough time in the past doing what pagans choose to do—living in debauchery, lust, drunkenness, orgies, carousing and detestable idolatry" (1 Peter 4:3, NIV). The time to stop is now.

Homosexuality is another sin than can take people to eternal condemnation. This sin consists of having sexual relationships with a person of the same sex; that includes, having sexual attractions, fantasy, or lust toward people of the same sex. God is clear about this: "You are not to sleep with a man as with a woman; it is detestable" (Leviticus 18:22, HCSB). How do people fall into such sin? The word of God gives us a description of the spiritual condition of those who fall into homosexuality. "Wherefore God also gave them up to uncleanness through the lusts of their own hearts, to dishonor their own bodies between themselves: Who changed the truth of God into a lie, and worshiped and served the creature more than the Creator, who is blessed forever. Amen. For this cause God gave them up unto vile affections: for even their women did change the natural use into that which is against nature" (Romans 1:24-26). As we can see in these verses, homosexuality begins with indifference toward God, which results in idolatry: those that are involved in homosexuality are worshiping the creatures rather than the Creator. Some people do not get to consummate the act, but they speak, walk, or behave in ways that are not consistent with the sex that God assigned to them when He created them; the Word calls them effeminate, which is also a sin.

But those that are in homosexuality and want to abandon it; what should they do? As with any other sin, we need to recognize it, and repent. In addition, we need to stop any activity, conversation, or relationship that represents a temptation or that entices that desire. We shall also eliminate any apparel, hair style, social network, or anything that is associated with that sinful behavior. If you have been hiding this sin, you need to renounce to the secret by speaking with someone that is spiritually sound and mature. The Scripture says, "But have renounced the hidden things of dishonesty…" (2 Corinthians 4:2). If we try to justify that sin because of what the world is saying, we will suffer the due punishment which comes from God. Many would say that we should not judge those who are practicing or other sins, and they are right; the word of God says that God will judge them

(Hebrews 13:4). But we need to tell the truth so that many can be saved and escape damnation. Do not be deceived; it does not matter how much people try to make it seem normal, God sees homosexuality as sin and He is the Judge. We can repent now. The word of God denounces sin, not just to make us feel guilty but for us to repent.

Let us observe these verses: "Know ye not that the unrighteous shall not inherit the kingdom of God? Be not deceived: neither fornicators, nor idolaters, nor adulterers, nor effeminate, And such were some of you: but ye are washed, but ye are sanctified, but ye are justified in the name of the Lord Jesus, and by the Spirit of our God" (1 Corinthians 6:9-11). These verses contain a vast list of sins. But what is fascinating about this Scripture is that it says that 'such were some of you: but you have now been washed and sanctified.' This means that Paul was speaking with Christians that used to practice those sins in the past, but that were washed and sanctified by God. That is what God does with those who repent. He tells us what is wrong and gives us the solution. There is forgiveness in Jesus if we repent with all our heart. Let us repent because the wrath of God is against all those who commit sinful acts (Romans 1:18-27).

There is one more thing regarding homosexuality that will affect people in this world. Those in such relationships will not be able to procreate or to give birth to children. When that happens, your generation will be extinguished. That is the desire and the agenda of the devil; he came to kill, steal, and destroy. But Jesus came so that we might have eternal and abundant life, and that includes having your own children. God wants us to reproduce and to have descendants, God's way is the best way: "For this cause shall a man leave his father and mother, and shall be joined unto his wife, and they two shall be one flesh" (Ephesians 5:31). Receive this word and act upon it in the name of Jesus.

Lack of Forgiveness: Another sin that will send many to hell is lack of forgiveness. Refusing to forgive will cause many Christians to lose salvation. Many Christians are holding grudges, personal resentment, anger, or bitterness towards people due to past injuries or offenses. When we do that we continue to press charges in our heart against that person, even after the person has repented. We need to remember that if we do not forgive; our Heavenly Father will not forgive us. (Matthew 6:15). What we need to do instead, is to call out the brother or sister who has committed the offense against us to try to make the person recognize their error. We do not do that for ourselves but to give our brother or sister an opportunity to repent, so that they can be saved. (Matthew 18:15-17).

There is a direct relation between forgiving and being forgiven by our Heavenly Father. Therefore, forgiving and remaining saved cannot be separated (Matthew 6:15). Moreover, when we hide grudges against others we can become bitter; and bitterness can also cause a believer to lose the grace. This is what the Scripture declares regarding bitterness: "Looking diligently lest any man fail of the grace of God; lest any root of bitterness springing up trouble you, and thereby many be defiled" (Hebrews

12:15). We know that we are saved by grace, so we cannot afford to lose grace if we want to remain saved.

Rebellion: Another sin that can take sons and daughter to hell is rebellion against parents; although, rebellion can affect anyone. The word of God says that we need to obey and to honor our father and mother to have a long and good life on earth (Ephesians 6:1-3). Those who disrespect they parents, both in words and actions are in great danger. Rebellion resides in the heart and many times people will not notice it. Remember that God sees what is in the heart because He searches the heart. (Jeremiah 17:10).

Sin of omission: is to fail to do what is good and right. Therefore, abstaining from doing good works is sin (James 4:17). The sin of omission is very subtle. Many will be caught committing this sin because it does not look as bad as other sins. But Jesus wanted to make sure that we understand the consequences of ignoring the needs of our brothers and sisters when we have the power to help. That is why Jesus gave us a preview of the future. Jesus is saying that at the end there will be only two groups of people; and each group will be standing before Him. One group will be at His left hand and the other group at His right. "Then he will say to those on his left, 'Depart from me, you who are cursed, into the eternal fire prepared for the devil and his angels" (Matthew 25:41). Anyone would expect to hear a list of terrible sins committed by this group; however, this list could surprise anyone: "For I was hungry and you gave me nothing to eat, I was thirsty and you gave me nothing to drink, I was a stranger and you did not invite me in,

I needed clothes and you did not clothe me, I was sick and in prison and you did not look after me" (Matthew 25:41-43, NIV). All that this group did was to do nothing. We got to be careful; we could be sent to the eternal fire for doing nothing! If you take another look to the group of the left, these were believers! How do we know that? We know that because of the reply that they gave to Jesus: they said, Lord when did we see you in these needs and did not help you? They called Him Lord; they were trying to impress the Lord by showing concern about their failure of identifying Him when he was in need. Which Jesus replied to saying: when you did not do it to one of these little ones you did not do it to me. This sin does not look like something drastic; it can be easily ignored, and even forgotten. But not by Jesus; He will remember. We could pretend that we did not know about the need of our brothers and sisters, but God knows that we knew.

Remember that the rich man was guilty of ignoring Lazarus' needs and went directly to a place of torment after he died. Perhaps, the greatest surprise of this scripture is the fact that Jesus showed no sympathy toward the apparent innocence of this group; He sends them directly to the fire. I want to emphasize something: Jesus will not be in His role of Savior at that occasion. He will be in His role of Judge. And as a judge He will not be compassionate; He will just follow what is written. The time to find mercy is now! We are warned so that we do not end up in the group on the left. We can choose now to keep doing what is right, to keep hold of our salvation to be able to stand at the right hand of God. We shall not waste the sacrifice that Christ made on our behalf. Jesus specified that hell was not prepared for humans but for the devil and his angels. However, humans go there by choice. The devil and his angels already made their choice. But we still have time to choose right. That is why God has given us opportunities to choose ever since the Garden of Eden. Centuries later God also started to give choices to the people of Israel, and He is doing the same with us today. Let us choose to obey Him so that we may live forever in His presence.

Teaching False Doctrines:

This sin can take people to perdition quickly. False teachers will send many to hell, and they will also perish. What makes a teacher a false teacher? Someone who knows the truth but does not teach it because of selfish ambition is a false teacher. There are many reasons why many are teaching things that are contrary to the word of God. One of those reasons is finance. These leaders are concerned about their income. They are commercializing the gospel because of covetousness. Others are watering down the message because of their love of fame. Some of these leaders have experienced great moments in the spotlight. They have earned a great reputation in the media and are liked by the masses. But one day every leader will be challenged. Someone will ask a question; they know that if they answer in a way that would honor God they could lose their great reputation. They know that they can fall in disgrace before the public. Many would pretend to be better than Jesus by preaching a watered-down gospel to accommodate Christians and non-Christians alike. Those teachers prefer to be a curse rather than standing for what is right. Why are they a curse; because the Scripture says that those who preach another gospel be accursed. (Galatians 1:8). Those are the ones that are educating people while neglecting their souls. We must be careful in not doing the works of the ministry because of selfish ambitions. In some ministries Jesus was kicked out a long time ago. Those teachers will suffer a punishment relative to their degree of knowledge (James 3:1). Those people introduce wrong teachings subtly. "But there were also false prophets among the people, just as there will be false teachers among you. They will secretly introduce destructive heresies, even denying the sovereign Lord who bought them—bringing swift destruction on themselves" (2 Peter 2:1, NIV). They will experience destruction for their sins for teaching what is not right. God has no pleasure in wickedness, and evil will not dwell with Him. (Psalm 5:4).

There are many other sins that I could mention but the word of God gives us a rule to be able to identify what constitutes a sin. The Scripture says that all unrighteousness is sin (1 John 5:17). That is why the Word also says that the unrighteous will not inherit the kingdom of God. We need to think and act in justice to be more like our Heavenly Father.

The Correct Attitude of Christians towards Sin

As Christians we are called to avoid even speaking about the sinful acts that others commit. "For it is a shame even to speak of those things which are done of them in secret" (Ephesians 5:12). That includes those sinful acts that are portrayed in movies, and other programs that can be seen on the screen, on magazines, social networks, and more. The Scripture says, "But fornication, and all uncleanness, or covetousness, let it not be once named among you…" (Ephesians 5:3).

Chapter Summary:

- Sin, whether it is in thoughts or actions, whether it is a sin of omission or commission can lead one to lose salvation. We need to abandon sin. All injustice is sin.

- There will be a day that God will judge every believer based on what they did to mitigate the needs of other believers. We need to be very careful because it is very easy to commit this type of sin. Not helping others can take us to perdition. Jesus will not be on His role of Savior in that day. He will be acting as the Judge. The time to find mercy is now.

- Through a genuine repentance one can move on and live a holy life. A genuine repentance happens when the believer does not want to repeat the same offense again, like King David did.

- We all have sinned against God in many ways. The time to repent is now. If you want to ask God to forgive you, repeat this prayer:

"Heavenly Father, I am sorry for sinning against You. I know that You hate sin because You Are Holy. But Your Word says that if I confess my sins You are faithful and just to forgive me (1 John

1:9). (Mention any specific sin that comes to your mind right now). Please forgive me Lord, and cleanse me with the precious blood of Jesus. This I pray in the Almighty name of Jesus. Amen."

Now, start living a fruitful life of obedience and holiness before God. And always give Him the first place in your life.

Chapter 6

CAN I TAKE MY OWN LIFE AND STILL GO TO HEAVEN?

Many spiritual leaders are blessing suicide among believers. They are doing so by assuring the believers that they will not lose their salvation by ending their lives. Be careful, the enemy is trying to make people believe that they can have an easy gospel. But many ignore that such a gospel can cost them everything: even their souls. Those who are teaching O.S.A.S. are introducing a hidden message of eternal death within their teachings. In the secular world, any law enforcement agent, or any ordinary individual would do anything to prevent someone from committing suicide. You might have heard about a case where a total stranger impeded someone from committing suicide.

People even risk their own lives to save a desperate individual from committing such act because they understand that suicide is a terrible and irrevocable decision. But what about when a spiritual leader is teaching the believers that is okay to end their lives! They teach a troubled believer that he or she will not lose their salvation by committing suicide! When someone is desperate that is all he needs to hear before going and committing that act. That assurance from a spiritual leader is viewed by the distressed individual as an endorsement of suicide. That is very dangerous, and is becoming epidemic. Watch carefully what is being preached today. That is the most dangerous aspect, and the real agenda of the teaching of Once Saved Always Saved. That agenda is of the devil who came to kill, steal, and destroy. Do not be deceived. But praise to God for Jesus our Lord Who came to give us eternal life and abundant life. That is why I am writing to help you receive or retain the gift of salvation that Jesus purchased for you. Let's continue to study O.S.A.S. more deeply so that you can have more tools to unmask, and dismantle this deadly teaching.

Suicide Makes Christians Lose Reward or Salvation?

The word of God is clear regarding tainting the Gospel, "But even if we or an angel from heaven should preach a gospel other than the one we preached to you, let them be under God's curse! …If anybody is preaching to you a gospel other than what you accepted, let them be under God's curse" (Galatians 1:8-9, NIV). False teachings bring curses because it is a different gospel. I believe that suicide is a direct curse that derives from the false gospel of Once Saved Always Saved. The believers are being told that they can commit suicide and still, remain saved because nothing can make them lose salvation. To support this false teaching, they explain that the only consequence that the believer may face after committing suicide is to lose rewards. This doctrine does not contemplate the idea that a Christian can lose salvation; however, the word of God clearly teaches that salvation can be lost as we have observed in this book. Jesus took time during His ministry to teach about the reasons why some Christians would lose salvation. Here are more proofs: "Then he will say to those on his left, 'Depart from me, you who are cursed, into the eternal fire prepared for the devil and his angels'" (Matthew 25:41). In the following verses Jesus continues to explain the reasons why those individuals are going to be sent to the eternal fire.

By now let us take a closer look at the fact that those that were at the left hand of Jesus were believers. How do we know that? We know that because they called Jesus Lord. They were very kind and humble when they were presenting their excuses before Jesus. They even expressed great concern about having missed an opportunity to serve their Lord. Also, they seemed not to be ignorant regarding the Christian life and the Christian language. Furthermore, the Lord expected them to care for the need of the little ones. Jesus would not do that with people that despise Him. This is not a judgment for atheists or people that don't accept Jesus as Lord and Savior. These were Christians that failed to do what was right. They were not great sinners; in fact, they thought that they would be allowed into heaven. Now, let's see the reason why they lost their salvation. This is how Jesus describes their sin: "For I was hungry and you gave me nothing to eat, I was thirsty and you gave me nothing to drink" (Matthew 25:43). They were punished for not doing what they were expected to do. And it is amazing how Jesus showed no mercy for them. This is serious my friend.

Now, I want to connect that group and their punishment to the reality of suicide among Christians. We can see how Jesus did not hesitate to send them to the fire. Then, how can a preacher be telling the believers that they will enter heaven if they decide to end their lives? How could they be giving assurance to the believers that they will not perish if they commit suicide? Jesus is showing us in advance what is going to take place in the future.

We need to remember that in that day, Jesus will not be relating to people as Savior; Jesus will be in His role of Judge. And we know that a just judge will send criminals to jail. We should not expect that Jesus will behave as a corrupt judge breaking the law to favor anyone. Think about this: If Jesus sent to the fire those who did not do what was right, He will not exonerate those who do what is wrong, those who commit murder against themselves. Life is for God to give and to take. Please pay attention and you will see that this judgment is not a judgment for rewards. Jesus made it very clear that this judgment was for salvation and condemnation. The group on the right was invited into the kingdom of the Father, while the group on the left was sent to the eternal fire prepared for the devil and his angels

(Matthew 25:41). This judgment has eternal consequences. This is not a reward ceremony. Jesus wanted to make sure that we know what will happen so that we can make the choices now to be on His right hand. Suicide will put people on the left side.

There is Memory in Hell

The person who commits suicide will open his eyes in the place of torment and will remember everything that happened in his life. The Scripture reveals that there is a clear memory of this life in hell. People remember their loved ones and don't want them to go there. Do not be deceived by a teaching that is trying to paint suicide as an alternative to a life full of turmoil. Suicide is murder, and murderers have not eternal life. "Whosoever hateth his brother is a murderer: and ye know that no murderer hath eternal life abiding in him" (1 John 3:15). I am using this Scripture on purpose to let you see that God will not give eternal life to the person who commits murder, even if it is committed in the heart. Just by hating someone, people will not be allowed to enter heaven, imagine those who kill themselves.

God is good and merciful; He is also righteous and faithful to His word; He will not alter His word. Remember the rich man in the story that Jesus told; how Abraham treated the rich man. Abraham was firm and did not grant any of his requests; not even for Lazarus to dip the tip of his finger in water to refresh his lips from the flames. Abraham kindly, but firmly reminded him about the decisions that he had made in the world: "But Abraham said, Son, remember that thou in thy lifetime receivedst thy good things, and likewise Lazarus evil things: but now he is comforted, and thou art tormented" (Luke 16:25). And when the rich man asked for Lazarus to be sent to his relatives, Abraham recommended the word of God for his relatives: "…They have Moses and the prophets; let them hear them (Luke 16:29). By mentioning Moses and the prophets, Abraham was clearly referring to the Scriptures. When the rich man—very poor now—persisted for Lazarus to be sent to preach to his relatives, Abraham replied: "…If they hear not Moses and the prophets, neither will they be persuaded, though one rose from the dead" (Luke 16:31). In other words, Abraham was implying that if someone does not believe what the word of God says, he will not be convinced even by experiencing something supernatural.

We need to trust everything that the word of God says and that includes what it says about salvation, heaven and hell. How can a preacher be telling the people that God will allow them into heaven if they decide to break the law of God that says do not kill? This scripture allows us to see in advance the destiny of those who are lost because they made the wrong decisions in life. We can clearly see how things are handled after death. Whatever we decide here in this life is what we will find in eternity. We cannot decide something here and then expect a different result over there. It is established for men to die once and then face judgment (Hebrews 9:27). We should not be under the assumption that God will change His mind about our destiny. God does not move by feelings but by what is written in His word. God has provided His Son Jesus. Jesus has shed every drop of His precious blood to save us. But once we leave this world, it is over. There will not be another opportunity for repentance. God is not going to have a different standard for us, or to give us a second chance.

God is not going to be moved by suffering. Remember that the rich man was simply asking for the wet tip of Lazarus' finger and his request was denied. But that did not happen because of cruelty. Remember that Abraham told the rich man that there was a great gulf fixed between them which they could not cross. That gulf that separates those that are lost from those that are saved is made here in this life; and cannot be crossed after death. Thus, God did not change the rules, not even to quench the thirst of the rich man. God does not act like some people do; they are willing to break the rules to favor one of their own even if it is at the expense of others. If God were to act that way He would be using the methods of the devil, and that will never happen. That is another reason why we can fully trust God. He will do what He has said that He will do. We need to obey what He has said. The Lord had also given us commands regarding what not to do. He has said not to kill and that includes not killing ourselves.

They Are a Bad Example

There are three people in the Bible who committed suicide. They are King Saul, Ahithophel, and Judas. Let's begin by speaking about Saul. The word of God said that King Saul was disobedient to God; so much so, that he went to consult a witch after he had expelled the witches from the land. Saul killed himself that same day that he consulted the witch and had to face the consequences of his disobedience. The word of God is very specific about the decision that Saul made; and there is no suggestion that he found any mercy. "so Saul died for his transgression which he committed against the Lord, even against the word of the Lord, which he kept not, and also for asking counsel of one that had a familiar spirit, to enquire of it" (1 Chronicles 10:13).

Another person to commit suicide in the Bible was Ahithophel. Ahithophel committed suicide perhaps motivated by his pride, and his bitterness towards King David (2 Samuel 17:23). Ahithophel was the grandfather of Bathsheba the woman with whom King David committed adultery. In 2 Samuel 11:3 the Scripture provides the name of the father of Bathsheba, Eliam. In 2 Samuel 23:34 we find that Eliam was the son of Ahithophel. Therefore, when King David committed adultery with Ahithophel' granddaughter, Ahithophel must have been very affected. This seems to be the reason why he became part of the rebellion of Absalom against his father David. During the rebellion Ahithophel devised a perfect plan to kill David. His thirst for revenge was so strong that he planned to go in person to persecute David (2 Samuel 17:1). His counsel was so perfect that Ahithophel expected that it would be approved by Absalom. Nevertheless, God caused that his wise counsel be canceled in response to David's prayer. When Ahithophel saw that his plan was not approved, and that he would not be able to take revenge on David, he went back to his house and hanged himself.

Another person in the Bible that ended his life was Judas. When we think about who Judas was and the sin that he committed, we would not want to be associated with him or to repeat the same sin that he committed. Judas is the person who committed the greatest sin, which was to betraying Jesus. He conspired with the Pharisees to kill the Giver of Life. After committing such a horrendous act Judas hanged himself.

Suicide Eliminates the Opportunity for Repentance

As we have seen, Saul, Ahithophel, and Judas were in great distress and for this reason they decided to end their lives. But their real problems for them began after committing suicide. Because, by ending their lives they were also ending their opportunity for salvation. The word of God says, "do not kill." Suicide is to commit murder against self. Be careful, suicide is the only type of sin that does not allow an opportunity for repentance of the sinner because after committing that sin the person will be dead. And a dead person cannot repent.

My dear reader, by tempting people to end their lives the enemy is trying to destroy any opportunity for repentance. It does not matter how difficult your situation looks right now, you can continue to obey that commandment of God that says do not kill. When we decide to obey we find peace. Anything in this life can be overcome. But suicide is not the solution. Suicide will cause people to suffer eternally in hell. Whatever you are going through right now, bring it to Jesus. Pray about it, and leave it in God's hands. Speak with someone, don't keep it to yourself, and do not commit suicide.

Disobedience Can Lead to Desperation

Repeated disobedience to the word of God can take Christians to desperation. And when someone is desperate, they are vulnerable to the temptations of the enemy to end their lives. For example, King Saul was disobedient to the word of God since the beginning. He continued to do so until he became desperate. And when he got really desperate, he disobeyed the word of God even more! He consulted a witch to try to force God to give him an answer. Remember that God had given Saul many instructions, but he never followed them, so why would God give him anymore? That is why it is so important that we read the word of God to obey it. King Saul was in distress but there were many other believers in the Bible who experienced worse circumstances than he did but did not disobey God, much less ended their lives. Remember the afflictions of Job; he was so frustrated that desired to die and even cursed the day that he was born! (Job Chap.3).

Another case of desperation can be observed in the life of Judas. He had the opportunity of his life. Judas was hearing—but not listening— to the sermons of Jesus every day; he even received authority to rebuke devils! (Luke 9:1-6). However, Judas did not repent. After betraying Jesus, he did not beg for God's mercy. When he got too desperate he preferred to try to solve the problem by himself, so he ended his life. He was not accustomed to depending on the words of Jesus. As we can see these men did not depend on the word of God to solve their problems. I would like to know, when a preacher is telling the people that they are saved even if they commit suicide, are they trying to compare the believers to the three worse people in the Bible? Are they using Saul, Ahithophel, and Judas as references to assure the believers that they will be saved? These three men committed suicide in the Bible and are the worst examples of what a Christian should be. And remember that God will not change the rules to save anyone. And if you think that these men got lost because they were really bad people, think about the rich man who went to a place of torment. He was not a great sinner. He did not do anything wrong. His only sin was not to perform good deeds. The rich man seemed to live an average life; like many of us; he was only thinking about himself. But when he got to the place of torment his perception totally changed, but it was too late. He did not find any favor. He had to face the inexorable consequences of what he had decided while he was alive.

Your Life It Is Precious to God

You are alive; and because you are alive you can repent. You can start again. Even if you have lost your business, properties, or wealth; material things can be restored. The only thing that God will not restore is your life if you decide to end it. Perhaps, you may have lost a loved one such as a husband or wife, children, or friends; God can heal your heart. He will also bring new people to your life to give you some comfort in the middle of your circumstances. You can also be a blessing to others by sharing the compassion, and the understanding that you have gained from that experience. If you have lost your health and are in a sick bed, God can heal you, but even if you do not receive your healing right now, do not end your life. God is the One Who knows how long you are going to live. Leave that to God. Many had suffered in the Bible, but they decided to endure. Remember Lazarus? He had a terrible life. Lazarus was poor, homeless, and sick but he did not end his life. And because he did not end his life, when it was time for him to die he went immediately to enjoy eternity with God where he was comforted, and cared for. Do not end your life. Live!

If you have been battling with suicidal thoughts, you can repent right now. Ask God to forgive you for sinning in your heart. Remember that to God, sin can take place even in the heart. Repent from all your heart as King David did. Read Psalms 51.

Now Please repeat these words right now: "I will not die, but shall live and declare the works of the Lord" (Psalms 118:17). Continue to repeat that Scripture every day, and live to please God, in the mighty name of Jesus!

Chapter 7

WATCH THE TEACHING AND THE TEACHERS

False Doctrines and the Character of Leaders

Exposing and refuting a false doctrine is not complete until we unmask the character of those who teach them. The truth is that every false doctrine is developed by a person who decides to follow the lies of the enemy. We know that the first falsifier of the truth was satan. He entered the garden and began to twist the instructions that God has given to the men. But since the enemy

97

was exposed and punished, now he uses people to continue to distort the word of God; thus, he uses the false teachers. Please notice, that false doctrines begin where there are believers that are sincere, respectful, and faithful, but that are also inexpert in the word of God. The false teachers can turn those good qualities of the believers into allegiance to themselves. The teachers begin to mix the word of God with their opinions. They continue to teach big lies with great authority until the believers give more credit to their words than to the word of God. Consequently, false teachings are directly related to the character and practices of those who teach them. Their teachings spring from their hypocrisy, lack of fear God, and abundance of ambition. Jesus pointed to the hypocrisy of the Pharisees as the reason for their wrong behavior and manipulation of the people of God. Therefore, Jesus exposed their motives, and warned the believers saying: "Beware ye of the leaven of the Pharisees, which is hypocrisy" (Luke 12:1). There is hypocrisy in those who teach false beliefs because they know for sure that what they are teaching is not true. But they continue to teach it because they want fame, money, and power. "But there were false prophets also among the people, even as there shall be false teachers among you, who privily shall bring in damnable heresies, even denying the Lord that bought them, and bring upon themselves swift destruction" (2 Peter 2:1).

The following excerpt is from my book titled, *Faith: Heaven's Currency – The Duality of Faith.* Here you will find more biblical warnings about false teachers and some instructions in how to avoid being deceived by them. I pray that you are blessed by these words and that you can share them with someone who may need these words.

"One Last Warning: Beware of False Leaders

There is one more warning regarding the last days, and it is about the character of the people. The word of God says that, "People will be lovers of themselves, lovers of money, boastful, proud, abusive, disobedient to their parents, ungrateful, unholy, without love, unforgiving, slanderous, without self-control, brutal, not lovers of the good, treacherous, rash, conceited, lovers of pleasure rather than lovers of God— having a form of godliness but denying its power…" (2 Timothy 3:1-5, NIV). The most dangerous part of this warning is that these people have an appearance of godliness. That Scripture is referring to religious leaders who use hypocrisy to deceive innocent Christians that truly love the Lord. How do I know that this scripture refers to religious leaders? Because it says that they have an appearance of godliness, but with their actions they deny its power. That is dangerous because these people operate within the church; they hide under the name of a ministry. They may be pastors, leaders, apostles, deacons, or evangelists. Be careful!" (De La Rosa, 2017, pp. 122-123).

"How to Identify These False Leaders

"These leaders can be easily identified by observing what they do, not what they say. … Jesus also told us that by their fruits we shall know them (Matthew 7:20). The fruit that

Jesus is referring to is the fruit of the Spirit which is love, joy, peace, long-suffering, gentleness, goodness, faith, meekness, temperance, or self-control (Galatians 5:22-2). Compare the character of your leaders to see if it reflects the fruit of the Spirit. Take time to observe their actions. And if you find that their character has only an appearance of godliness, if they look more like the people described in 2 Timothy 3:1-5, Flee! Those leaders are lover of themselves, money (2 Timothy 3:2, 4). Regarding them we are given one specific instruction: Stay away from them (2 Timothy 3:5). Why should we stay away from them? We should stay away from them because those leaders manipulate people through their words and simulations. They want total submission from the people, and the believers who are accustomed to honoring the men and women of God will easily submit to those deceivers thinking that they are dealing with real people of God; but real people of God do not seek to take advantage, to control, or to rule over the people that are under their care." (De La Rosa, 2017, p. 123).

"Apostle Peter humbly warns pastors about this temptation as someone who had been under the tender care of the Shepherd of shepherds, Jesus Himself. "Feed the flock of God which is among you, taking the oversight thereof, not by constraint, but willingly; not for filthy lucre, but of a ready mind; Neither as being lords over God's heritage, but being examples to the flock" (1Peter 5:2-3). Please remember, Jesus does not want you to submit to the manipulation of such leaders; that's why He gives you this warning. Cutting out any relationship with them is the only way to escape their influence and hypocrisy. Those religious leaders do not obey God; much less, would they care for God's people. So, you should have no contact with them in obedience to what your Heavenly Father has instructed you" (De La Rosa, 2017, p. 123).

"Let's be ready to receive our Lord Jesus; He will faithfully return, and He will take us to the mansions that He has prepared for us. That can happen at any moment. My dear friend, if you have been a bit careless, if you are not sure that you are ready to meet Jesus if He were to come right now, please repeat this prayer: 'Father, I am sorry for sinning against You. You are a Holy God. Please forgive me. I believe that Jesus Christ died for me, and that He was raised from the dead, (Romans 10:9) and that He is sitting at Your right hand. Please forgive me Lord, and cleanse me with the precious blood of Jesus. This I pray in the almighty name of Jesus, Amen.' Now, start living in obedience and holiness before God, always giving Him the first place in your life (De La Rosa, 2017, p. 124)

Can Blood Be in the Hands of Teachers?

During his farewell speech to the believers, Apostle Paul said the following words: "Wherefore I take you to record this day, that I am pure from the blood of all men. For I have not shunned to declare unto you all the counsel of God" (Acts 20:26-27). Paul knew that as teacher of the word of God he was responsible for the blood of those who were listening to his teaching. He emphasized that he was pure or free from their blood because he had not refused to teach the whole counsel of the word of God. My dear brother or sister, if we fail to teach the whole truth of the Gospel we are putting blood in our hands; it is as simple as that. This is very dangerous before God. Blood in the hands means that if we don't teach the whole gospel people that are under our care could be lost. We need to remember to care for our salvation and for the salvation of others. When we observe how Apostle Paul conducted himself, we will see that he did not take his role as teacher very lightly. Paul was working and conducting his whole life as someone who will give account before God; for himself and for the people.

May the Lord guide you and give you the grace to live always ready to meet Him. I want to remind you about a determinant truth in the name of Jesus:

"Always pay attention to what is the most valuable thing in life: The salvation of your soul."

About the Author

Jose De La Rosa

Is the Overseer of World Christian Center, in the state of Georgia, USA. At a very young age, he graduated the Biblical Institute of Church of God, in the Dominican Republic and immediately started to serve as a worship leader and later as a pastor. He earned credits at the Gordon-Conwell Theological Seminary in Boston, MA and became a business man for more than twenty years while serving in ministry part-time before being anointed as an Apostle in 2006 and returning to full-time ministry in 2008. He is the author of *Faith: Heaven's Currency*, and *The Blessing Knows*.

World Christian Center
1620 Buford Hwy Suite 113 Buford GA 30518
Email: info@faithpublishers.com

Bibliography

De La Rosa, Jose. *Faith: Heaven's Currency -The Duality of Faith.* Buford:
    www.faithpublishers.com, 2017.

Made in the USA
Las Vegas, NV
12 April 2023

70501508R00066